PA-38 Tomahawk
A Pilot's Guide

Jeremy M. Pratt

Aviation Supplies & Academics, Inc.
Newcastle, Washington

U.S. Edition 1995

©1995 Aviation Supplies & Academics, Inc.

First published in England by Airplan Flight Equipment, Ltd.
and Jeremy M. Pratt, 1992

PA-38 Tomahawk: A Pilot's Guide
Jeremy M. Pratt

ASA-PG-PA-38
ISBN 1-56027-216-3

Aviation Supplies & Academics, Inc.
Newcastle, Washington

Printed in the United States of America

99 98 97 96 95   9 8 7 6 5 4 3 2 1

Library of Congress Cataloging-in-Publication Data:

Pratt, Jeremy M.
      PA-38 Tomahawk / Jeremy M. Pratt. — U.S. ed.
            p.   cm.   — (A pilot's guide)
      Includes index.
      ISBN 1-56027-216-3
      1. Piper PA-38-112 Tomahawk (Training plane)   I. Title.
      II. Series: Pratt, Jeremy M.   Pilot's guide.
      TL686.P5P733 1995
      629.132'5217—dc20   95-15209
                                                                                CIP

Acknowledgements

I would like to thank all those whose knowledge, help and advice went into this book; in particular:

Airspeed Aviation
Air Nova
Simon Booth
CAA Safety Promotion Section
CSE Aviation
Colourmatch
Adrian Dickinson
Steve Dickinson
David Hockings
Andy Holland
Phil Huntington

Wendy Mellor
Manchester School of Flying
Margaret Parkes
Paul Price
Ravenair
Neil Rigby
John Ross
Ian Sixsmith
John Thorpe
Visual Eyes

Sarah, Kate and Miles

Jeremy M. Pratt
August 1992

Contents

Section 3 – Handling the Piper PA-38 Tomahawk

Section 4 – Mixture and Carburetor Icing Supplement

Section 5 – Expanded PA-38 Pre-Flight Checklist

Section 6 – Loading and Performance

Section 7 – Conversions

Index

Editor's Note

Welcome to ASA's *A Pilot's Guide* series by Jeremy Pratt. In this guide, you'll learn from the experts the general principles involved in flying the PA-38 Tomahawk, with extra insight on individual characteristics gleaned from flying experience.

PA-38 Tomahawk: A Pilot's Guide is not an authoritative document. Material in this book is presented for the purposes of orientation, familiarization, and comparison only.

Performance figures are based upon the indicated weights, standard atmospheric conditions, level hard-surface dry runways, and no wind. They are values based upon calculations derived from flight tests conducted by the aircraft company under carefully documented conditions and using professional test pilots. Performance will vary with individual aircraft and numerous other factors affecting flight.

The approved *Pilot's Operating Handbook* and/or the approved *Airplane Flight Manual* is the only source of authoritative information for any individual aircraft. In the interests of safety and good airmanship, the pilot should be familiar with these documents.

Section 1
General Description

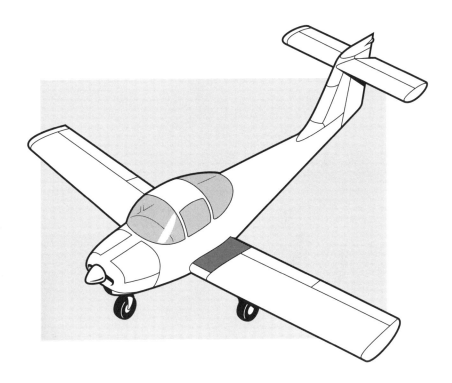

Introduction to the PA-38 Tomahawk

If a camel is a horse designed by a committee, then the Tomahawk is surely a trainer designed by instructors.

It was in the mid-1970s that Piper decided to build a true two-place trainer—their first since the high-wing, tube and fabric PA-22 Colt built in the early 1960s. An anonymous questionnaire was sent to 10,000 flight instructors, to determine the characteristics of their ideal trainer. The results make interesting reading: the top priorities included handling characteristics, performance, operating costs and cabin comfort; also preferred were features such as low noise level, the ability to spin and an easily accessible fuel selector.

Deliveries of the PA-38 Tomahawk began in 1978. Even a superficial look over the aircraft revealed the design philosophies it incorporated. The high aspect ratio, constant cord wing gives the appearance of being somewhat longer than its 34-foot span. The distinctive "T-tail"—the horizontal stabilizer perched at the top of the fin—helped give the aircraft its handling characteristics, and incidentally was very fashionable on light aircraft designed around this time. The two door cabin offered 360° visibility, easy access and comfortable accommodation. Some parts of the aircraft are interchangeable; i.e., main and nose wheels, left and right elevators, etc. The aircraft is powered by a Lycoming 4 cylinder air-cooled engine driving a fixed-pitch propeller.

The strength and operation of the door hinging and latching system attracted early comment, as did the "spring" elevator trim system. Most notably, perhaps, its stalling and spinning characteristics soon became a renowned feature of the Tomahawk.

In 1981, the Tomahawk II appeared. This model incorporated changes in response to several ADs (Airworthiness Directives) that had affected the original Tomahawk. In addition, items such as soundproofing and door latching were improved, and inboard wing flow strips (fitted on the wing leading edge to make the stall more docile) were incorporated. The most obvious external difference between the two versions are the 6.00 X 6 wheels fitted as standard on the Tomahawk II.

Production of the PA-38 Tomahawk ceased in 1983, largely as a result of the "product liability" situation that had made light aircraft manufacture uneconomical in the U.S. Just under 2,500 Tomahawks were produced in all.

MODEL YEAR	MODEL	PRODUCTION NAME
1978 – 1981	PA-38-112	Tomahawk

MODEL YEAR	MODEL	PRODUCTION NAME
1981 – 1982	PA-38-112	Tomahawk II

The Airframe

The PA-38 airframe is generally described as being of all-metal construction. The primary structure is constructed of aluminum alloy, with the engine mount and landing gear being made from steel. Some non-structural components such as the wing tips and landing gear fairings are made from fiberglass.

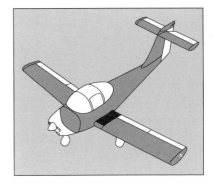

The fuselage has a semi-monocoque structure; that is, the vertical bulkheads and frames are joined by horizontal longerons and stringers which run the length of the fuselage. The metal skin is riveted to the longerons and stringers. This arrangement is conventional for modern light aircraft and allows loads to be spread over the whole construction. At the rear of the fuselage the tail unit incorporates a high "T-tail"—the horizontal stabilizer being mounted at the top of the fin assembly. Underneath the rear fuselage, a triangular combined tie-down point and tail guard is fitted.

The wings are of cantilever design (unsupported by external struts or bracing) and have a 5° dihedral. A main "I-bar" spar extending through the entire length of each wing is joined in the center of the fuselage with butt fittings. The spar is attached to each side of the fuselage and to the fuselage tunnel. An aft spar extends from wing tip to wing root and is joined to the fuselage side. On the upper surface of each wing a black walkway is marked. This is the only area of the wing to be walked on or stood on. Underneath each wing, a metal ring is installed to be used as a tie-down point. In the same area there is also a cone shaped protrusion which is used as a jacking point for maintenance operations.

The 5° positive dihedral is evident when the plane is viewed head-on.

The Flight Controls

Dual flight controls are installed as standard and link the cockpit controls to the control surfaces via cable and chain linkages. The controls are electrically bonded to the main airframe by means of bonding strips, and some surfaces have a static wick to dissipate static electricity to the atmosphere.

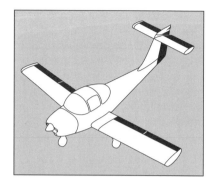

The AILERONS are of the differential type, moving upward through 26°, and downward through 14°. A balance weight is incorporated at the outer end of each aileron, inside the wing tip cavity.

The FLAPS are of the simple type, manually operated from a lever between the cockpit seats, through a torque tube and push rods to the flap surfaces. Three positions can be selected, fully up (0°), first stage (21°), and second stage—fully down—(34°). On some PA-38s the flaps do not lock in the fully up position and may droop or drop to the first stage when on the ground. The flap lever slot in the cockpit

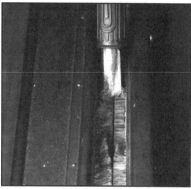

Flap lever slot with "brush."

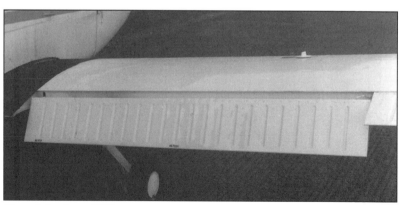

Flaps fully down (34°).

has a "brush" designed to stop objects falling into the cavity below. Unfortunately, there have been several incidents of pens, pencils, etc., falling through the brush and becoming tangled in the elevator cables. Some operators have fitted a guard around the flap lever; however, it is safest not to put any objects in this area at all.

The RUDDER is operated from the rudder pedals (which are also linked to the steerable nose wheel), and can move through 29° either side of the neutral position. On the trailing edge of the control surface a ground adjustable trim tab is fitted. Because the rudder is connected (via rods from the rudder pedals) to the nose wheel, the control surface cannot be moved while the aircraft is stationary without exerting considerable force—this is not recommended.

The ELEVATOR is fitted to the horizontal stabilizer on the "T-tail." The theory of the "T-tail" arrangement on light aircraft is that the horizontal stabilizer and elevator are mounted outside of the turbulent propeller slipstream and so give better handling characteristics. The control moves up through 34° and down through 20°, and incorporates a horn balance at the outer tip.

An adjustable TRIM system is incorporated into the elevator function. This is a spring-type control. Operation of the cockpit trim wheel acts on a spring, which in turn exerts a bias on the elevator control circuit. It is probably fair to say that this system does not give as positive a trim as many other types, and in some situations, it is possible to run out of "nose-up" trim. An indicator mounted next to the trim wheel shows the trim position setting. The control works in the natural sense; i.e., trimming the wheel forward gives nose down trim, and vice versa.

PA-38 Tomahawk tail unit.

The Landing Gear

The Tomahawk landing gear is fixed and is a tricycle-type, with a nose wheel rather than tailwheel.

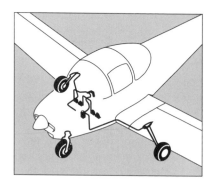

The main gear has a "leaf spring" steel landing gear strut which attaches to the main spar, with a fairing where the strut joins the lower wing surface. Although almost fragile in appearance, this arrangement is very strong—as you would expect on a training aircraft. However, there have been some problems where the bolts used in the attachment have failed in normal usage. There is a service bulletin relevant to this problem. The main gear has a 10-foot track—the distance between the two main wheels.

The nose gear attaches to the engine mount, and has an air/oil oleo strut to damp and absorb the normal operating loads. On the rear of the nose strut a torque link is installed to maintain the correct alignment of the nose wheel; the lower arm is fitted to the nose wheel fork, and the upper arm to the oleo cylinder casing. The nose gear is steerable through direct linkage to the rudder pedals. The nose wheel has a range of movement of 30° either side of dead ahead.

Main wheel unit.

Nose wheel assembly.

Brake disc and brake unit (main wheel).

Brake fluid reservoir.

The BRAKE system consists of single disc brake assemblies fitted to the main wheels and is operated by a hydraulic system. The brake lever in the cockpit operates a master cylinder located below and to the left of the throttle quadrant. When this control is pulled back, braking is evenly applied to both main wheels. A small button on the brake lever allows it to be locked in the ON position, to act as a parking brake. To release the parking brake the lever is pulled back, and then pushed to its forward limit. The button automatically disengages. When optional toe brakes are also installed, they are operated by depressing the upper half of the rudder pedal. In this system, each toe brake has a separate brake cylinder above the pedal, and it is possible to operate the brakes differentially—to the left or right wheel. This system allows the aircraft to turn in a very tight circle, and it is possible to lock one main wheel with the use of some pedal force. Turning around a wheel in this fashion tends to "scrub" the tire and is generally discouraged. A brake fluid reservoir is fitted to the upper left forward face of the firewall (accessed via the left engine cowling). Here it can be inspected for fluid level and replenished if necessary.

The landing gear is fitted with 5.00 X 5 tires as standard on the original Tomahawk. 6.00 X 6 tires are fitted as standard on the Tomahawk II, and were available as a option on the earlier aircraft. Both tires are of a four-ply tube type. The tire grooves should have at least 1/16 inch depth over 75% of the tire to be serviceable. Additionally, if the tread across the width of the tire is worn to less than 1/16 inch in any one place, the tire will need replacing.

The Engine

The Tomahawk is fitted with a Lycoming 0-235-L2C (Slick magnetos) or 0-235-L2A (Bendix magnetos); both versions are rated 112 HP at 2,600 RPM.

The engine is a four-cylinder unit, with cylinders horizontally opposed across the crankshaft. The cylinders are staggered so that each connecting rod has its own crankshaft throw. The cylinders and crankcase assembly are fashioned from aluminum alloy castings.

The engine is air-cooled. Airflow enters the engine compartment at the front of the cowling, and is directed by baffles to flow over the whole engine. The cylinders feature deep cooling fins that aid in engine cooling. The airflow leaves the engine compartment at the rear lower cowling underneath the engine compartment.

The engine is mounted on a steel tubular mounting which incorporates dynafocal insulators to reduce vibration. This mounting then attaches to the firewall. The mounting is designed to offset the engine center line several degrees to the right (as seen from the cockpit); this offsets the thrust line to help counteract the slipstream effect, which acts to the left.

Right-hand view of Lycoming 0-235 engine.

The Propeller

The propeller is an all metal, two bladed, fixed pitch design, turned by direct drive from the engine crankshaft. It rotates clockwise as seen from the cockpit.

The pitch is 56" (determined at 75% of the diameter) and the diameter is 72", with a minimum allowable diameter of 70".

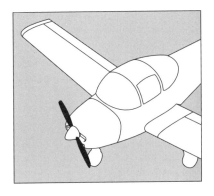

Slight offset of engine can be seen when the plane is viewed head-on.

The Ignition System

The engine features a dual ignition system, fitted with two Slick or Bendix magnetos. The magnetos are small AC generators which are driven by the crankshaft rotation to provide a very high voltage to a distributor, which directs it via high voltage leads (or high tension leads) to the spark plugs. At the spark plug the current must cross a gap; in doing so a spark is produced which ignites the fuel/air mixture in the cylinder.

The magnetos are fitted at the rear of the engine, one each side of the engine center line (hence, Left and Right magnetos). The usual arrangement is for each magneto to fire one spark plug in each cylinder. Each cylinder has two spark plugs (top and bottom) for safety and efficiency. The leads that run from the magnetos to the spark plugs should be secure, and there should be no splits or cracks in the plastic insulation covering the leads.

It is worth emphasizing that the ignition system is totally independent of the aircraft electrical system, and once the engine is running it will operate regardless of the serviceability of the battery or alternator.

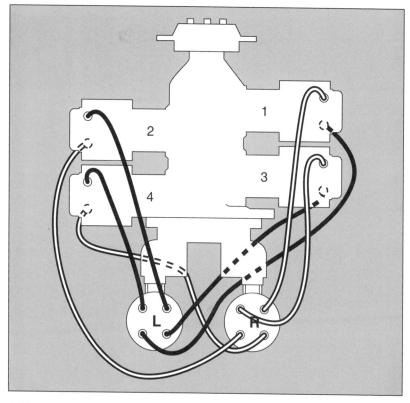

The Oil System

The engine's oil system provides lubrication, cooling, sealing, cleansing and protection against corrosion. It is a wet-sump, pressure-feed system. The oil sump is located under the engine, and oil is drawn from here by the engine-driven oil pump, through a filter and into the oil gallery of the crankcase. When the oil has flowed around the engine it drains down to the sump by gravity. The oil filter is mounted at the upper rear of the engine and is surrounded by a shroud, into which cooling air from the rear engine baffle is fed. An oil pressure relief valve is also installed, and its function is to maintain the correct operating pressure over a wide range of temperatures and RPM settings. Above a certain pressure, this valve will open and allow oil to return to the sump, rather than continuing into the lubricating system.

Oil filler tube.

Oil quantity can be checked on a dipstick on the right side of the engine. The dipstick is graduated in U.S. quarts and measures the quantity of the oil in the sump. When the engine has been running, the oil will take up to 10 minutes to return to the sump; only then can a true reading be taken. When replacing the dipstick, care should be taken not to overtighten the cap. To do so may make it exceptionally difficult to open the cap again, and it is possible to strip the thread on the cap or filler tube.

The oil temperature and oil pressure gauges in the cockpit are electrically operated and linked to a sender unit in the engine.

The Starter System

The starter motor is housed at the lower front left side of the engine. It incorporates a geared cog that engages with the teeth of the starter ring when the starter is operated. As the engine turns, an impulse coupling in the left magneto operates; this retards the spark and aids starting. When the engine fires and begins to rotate under its own power, this impulse coupling ceases to operate and normal spark timing is resumed. When the key is released, it returns to the BOTH position, and the cog on the starter motor withdraws to be clear of the starter ring.

The starter motor unit is just visible above the landing light.

The Fuel System

The Tomahawk has two aluminum fuel tanks, located in the inboard leading edge of each wing. From these tanks a fuel line runs through the wing and fuselage to the fuel selector valve. After this valve, the fuel line runs through the firewall to a fuel strainer bowl mounted on the forward left face of the firewall. Beyond the strainer bowl, a fuel line runs through the electric fuel pump and engine-driven fuel pump to the carburetor. A separate line runs from the strainer bowl to the cockpit primer and from there to the engine primer nozzles.

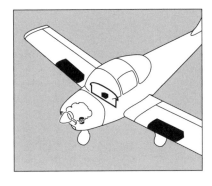

Each tank has a TANK VENT, a forward facing pipe on the lower inboard surface of the wing which ensures that ambient pressure is maintained above the fuel in the fuel tank. Should this vent become blocked, a vacuum may form in the tank as the fuel level lowers, and fuel flow to the engine may be interrupted.

There are three FUEL STRAINERS, one at the lower rear inboard edge of each tank, accessible from the inboard lower wing surface; and one from the fuel bowl, accessed at the lower left cowling. Fuel can only be drawn from the bowl if the cockpit fuel selector is in the LEFT or RIGHT position.

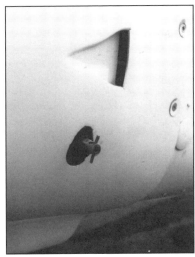

Engine fuel strainer.

Underwing fuel strainer.

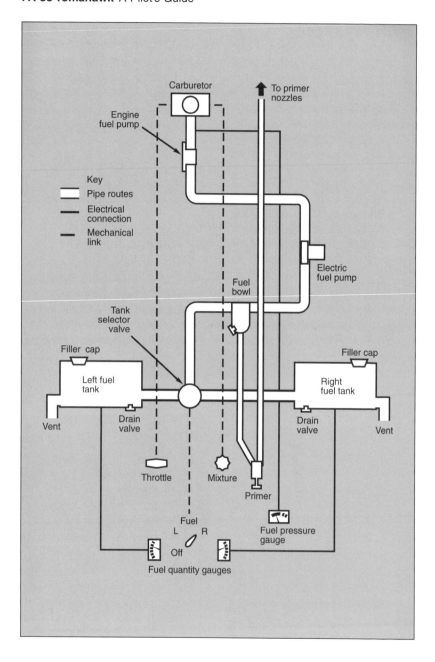

Cockpit fuel selector and throttle quadrant.

The cockpit FUEL SELECTOR is a popular feature of the Tomahawk. The selector is centrally located on the power quadrant and easily accessible to each pilot. The selector can be used to feed the engine from either the Left or Right tank. To turn the fuel off, a spring loaded latch next to the bottom of the selector lever must first be depressed, then the lever rotated to the OFF position. This operation can be a two handed operation, which does help prevent the accidental selection of the OFF position.

In normal operation, the fuel is drawn through the system by an engine-driven FUEL PUMP. However, should this pump fail, the fuel supply to the carburetor will cease and the engine will stop. Therefore, a second electric fuel pump is installed. This pump is selected ON or OFF from a cockpit switch. Normally the electric fuel pump is used during takeoff and landing, and when changing tanks. A fuel pressure gauge is installed that reads from a sender between the engine-driven fuel pump and the carburetor.

The Carburetor

The carburetor mixes air with the fuel from the fuel system and supplies the fuel/air mix to the cylinders. The carburetor is located under the engine, and takes induction air from a scoop intake in the lower front cowling. This air is filtered and then fed into the carburetor air box. In this box, a butterfly valve is used to allow either the induction air, or heated air, to be fed to the carburetor. Heated air comes from an unfiltered inlet inside the front cowling, then passes into a shroud around the exhaust, which heats it before it reaches the carburetor. Hot or cold air is selected by the carburetor heat control in the cockpit. The use of this control and the subject of carburetor icing are fully discussed in Section 4.

From the carburetor, the fuel/air mix is carried through a "center zone induction manifold"; that is, the mix is carried through the engine oil sump which heats it to ensure more uniform vaporization. This also aids in the cooling of the oil.

The primer control, situated to the right of the throttle quadrant, is an aid to starting. The control is unlocked by rotating the primer until a pin on the shaft aligns with the cut-out in the collar. The control can then be pulled out, filling the pump with fuel from the fuel bowl. The primer is then pushed in, delivering fuel to the primer nozzles. When priming is complete, the control should be pushed fully in with the pin aligned with the collar cut-out, and then rotated about half a turn. As a check, attempt to pull the primer out; it should remain locked. It is important that the primer is fully locked, otherwise engine rough-running may result.

The mixture is controlled from the MIXTURE lever located on the power quadrant in the cockpit which adjusts the fuel/air ratio in the carburetor. In the fully forward position it gives a RICH mixture, and if moved to the rearward ICO (Idle Cut-Off) position the fuel supply is cut off and the engine stops.

The power quadrant has a vertical wheel on the lower center edge. Movement of this "friction wheel" adjusts the friction that holds the throttle and mixture levers in position, allowing them to be locked in a desired position. Generally, this wheel is adjusted to leave the throttle and mixture with relatively loose and easy movement on the ground, but is tightened to hold the levers in position for takeoff.

The Electrical System

The Tomahawk has a 14 volt, direct current electrical system. The alternator is mounted to the front lower right of the engine and is engine driven from a belt drive and pulley directly behind the starter ring, The alternator is rated at 60 amps. A 12 volt, 25 ampere-hour battery is located inside a vented box on the upper forward right side of the firewall.

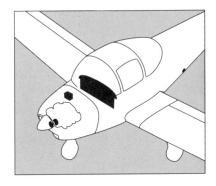

The ALTERNATOR is the primary source of power to the electrical system, in normal operations with the engine running. The alternator produces alternating current (AC), which is converted into direct current (DC) by diodes incorporated in the alternator housing, which act as rectifiers. By their design, alternators require a small voltage (about 3 volts) to produce the electromagnetic field required inside the alternator. The significance of this is that if the battery is completely discharged (flat), the alternator will not be able to supply any power to the electrical system, even after the engine has been started by some other means (i.e., external power or hand-propping). Output from the alternator is controlled by a VOLTAGE REGULATOR which is mounted behind the right-hand side of the instrument panel. An OVER-VOLTAGE RELAY located next to the voltage regulator protects the system from possible damage due to an overvoltage condition. In the event of an overvoltage of about 16.5V, the relay opens and the alternator is isolated from the electrical system.

The primary purposes of the BATTERY are to provide power for engine starting, the initial excitation of the alternator, and as a backup in the event of alternator failure. In normal operations with the engine running, the alternator provides the power to the electrical system and charges the battery. A fully-charged battery has a charging rate of about 2 amperes. In a partially discharged condition (i.e., just after engine start) the charging rate can be much higher than this. In the event of an alternator failure, the battery provides *all* power to the electrical system. In theory, a fully-charged 25 ampere-hour battery is capable of providing 25 amps for 1 hour, 1 amp for 25 hours, or 12.5 amps for 2 hours, etc. In practice, the power available is governed by factors such as battery age and condition, load placed on it, etc. In the case of an alternator failure while flying, the best advice is to reduce electrical load to the minimum consistent with safety, and plan to make a landing at the earliest opportunity.

The AMMETER, located in the engine instrument group to the right of the power quadrant, indicates in amperes the electrical load on the alternator. With the engine running and all electrical services turned off, the ammeter will indicate the charging rate of the battery. As services are switched on, the ammeter will indicate the additional load of each item. In the case of night flight, the maximum continuous load will be in the region of 30 amps. In the event of alternator failure, the ammeter will indicate zero, and where installed, a red "Low Voltage" warning light will illuminate.

The master switch (left) and electrical switches (right).

The pilot controls the electrical system by the MASTER SWITCH located on the left side of the instrument panel. This is a split rocker switch with two halves labeled BAT and ALT. Normally, the switch is operated as one, with both halves used together. The BAT half of the switch can be operated independently, so that all electrical power is being drawn from the battery only. However, the ALT side can only be turned on in conjunction with the BAT half. Should an electrical problem occur, the master switch can be used to reset the electrical system by turning it OFF for 2 seconds, and then turning it ON again.

The aircraft may be fitted with an EXTERNAL POWER RECEPTACLE in the right-hand fuselage behind the wing root. This can be used to connect external power for starting or operation of the aircraft electrical system. Before using external power, it is imperative to check that the external power unit is of the correct voltage—otherwise *serious damage could be inflicted on the electrical system*. Additionally, it should be remembered that if the

External power receptacle.

The low voltage warning light (bottom left) and alternator warning light (upper right).

battery is totally flat (completely discharged), it will need to be removed and recharged or replaced before flight.

To use external power, the following procedure should be adopted:

1. Check that master switch and all electrical equipment are OFF.

2. Ensure that the *red* lead of the jumper cable goes to the *positive* terminal of the external power source, and the *black* lead to the *negative*.

3. Insert the cable plug into the aircraft external power receptacle socket.

4. Turn the master switch ON, and proceed with normal starting procedure.

5. After engine start, turn master switch and all electrical equipment OFF and remove the cable plug.

6. Turn the master switch ON, and check the ammeter. If no output is shown, flight should not be attempted.

The various electrically-operated systems are protected by individual CIRCUIT BREAKERS, which are located in a cluster on the right lower instrument panel. Should a problem occur (e.g., a short circuit), the relevant circuit breaker may "pop," and will be raised in relation to the other circuit breakers (CBs). The correct procedure is to allow the CB to cool for 2 minutes, then reset it and check the result. If the CB pops again, it should not be reset. The alternator field has a 60 ampere CB, and the voltage regulator has a 5 ampere CB. All CBs show their rating and the components they protect.

Electrical fires are rare, but can be characterized by smoke in the cockpit and the distinctive smell of burning insulation. The PA-38 has been involved in incidents where faults in the internal electrical system have led to problems including smoke in the cockpit. In this case, the problem may be solved by isolating a circuit if a particular component is suspected (i.e., turning off the nav. lights if the smoke appeared after they were switched on), or by turning off the master switch to shut down the electrical system. In either case, it is prudent to land at the earliest opportunity.

Apart from engine starting and the alternator field, the electrical system supplies power to the following:

• All internal and external lights.

• All radios and intercom.

• Turn coordinator.

• Stall warning, Pitot heater, Electric fuel pump.

• Fuel gauges, Oil temperature gauge, Oil pressure gauge.

Circuit breaker panel.

The Stall Warning System

An audible alarm located behind the instrument panel is electrically activated from a stall warning vane on the leading edge of the left wing. This vane moves up at angles of attack approaching the stall, and gives a warning at approximately 5 to 10 knots above the stall speed. This vane can be checked before flight by gently moving the vane upwards with the master switch ON; the alarm should then be heard. With the master switch OFF, or with an electrical failure, the stall warning is inoperative.

Wing-mounted stall warning vane.

The Lighting System

The PA-38 may be equipped with a variety of optional internal and external lighting. A feature of most Tomahawks are the wing-tip "strobe" lights which act as anti-collision lights. As a general rule, the strobes are not used during taxiing because they can dazzle and distract those nearby. They are, however, very effective in the air. If flying in cloud conditions or heavy precipitation, it is recommended that they be turned off, as the pilot may become spatially disorientated.

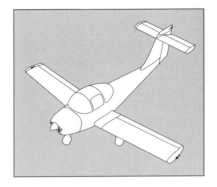

The landing light is fitted in the lower front nose cowling; it should be used with some discretion, not least because of the very short life of the light bulbs. Navigation lights are controlled from a switch on the lower right of the instrument panel, which also controls the instrument panel lighting. It is a rotatable rheostat-type switch. When the switch is first turned on, the navigation lights are illuminated at their set brilliance. The switch can be rotated to control the level of instrument panel lighting. The navigation lights remain at their set brightness until the switch is turned

Cockpit lighting controls.

fully off. Next to this switch, a similar switch controls just the radio panel lighting. There is also an overhead "dome" light located in the cabin ceiling; this light is of a set brightness and has a on/off switch located on its side.

The Vacuum System

An engine-driven vacuum pump is mounted to the upper rear face of the engine. This pump is fitted with a plastic shear drive, so that should the pump seize, the shear drive will fail and the engine will not be damaged. Air enters the vacuum system through a filter, passes through the air-driven gyro instruments (and is measured by the suction gauge). Then air flows through a vacuum regulator and into the vacuum pump, from which it is expelled through a short pipe.

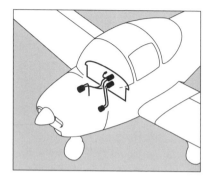

Suction is used to drive the gyros in the attitude indicator (or artificial horizon) and heading indicator (or direction indicator). A suction gauge mounted on the instrument panel measures suction; for cruising RPMs and altitudes, the reading should be 5.0 inches of mercury, +/-0.1 inches. At higher or lower settings, the gyros may become unreliable. A lower suction over an extended period may indicate a faulty vacuum regulator, dirty screens or a system leak. If the vacuum pump fails or a line collapses, the suction gauge reading will fall to zero, and the attitude indicator and heading indicator will become unreliable over a period of some minutes as the gyros run down, losing RPM. The real danger here is that the effect is gradual and may not be noticed by the pilot for some time.

The engine-driven vacuum pump.

The Pitot-Static System

The pitot-static system supplies static pressure to the vertical speed indicator (VSI) and altimeter, and static and pitot pressure to the airspeed indicator (ASI).

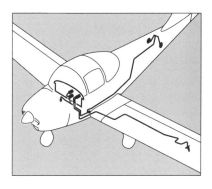

Pitot pressure comes from a PITOT TUBE which is located under the left wing. Static pressure comes from two STATIC VENTS located on the rear fuselage (one each side). The use of two static vents is designed to help alleviate position error and maneuver-induced error on the pressure instruments.

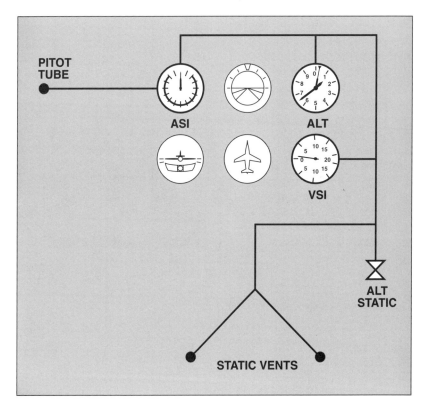

PITOT TUBE

ASI

ALT

VSI

ALT STATIC

STATIC VENTS

No checking system is incorporated in the system, and instrument indications in the event of a leak or blockage are outside the scope of this book. However, both the pitot tube and the static vents have back-up systems.

As an option, the pitot tube has a heating element, which is activated by a switch in the electrical rocker switch group in front of the pilot, labeled PITOT HEAT. Pitot heat can prevent blockage of the pitot tube in heavy rain or icing. This notwithstanding, it must be remembered that *the PA-38 is not cleared for flight into known icing conditions.*

The pitot tube.

An alternate static source is installed in the cockpit to be used in the case of failure or blockage of the normal static vents.

The external static vents should be checked before flight to ensure that they are clear and unobstructed. A similar check is carried out on the pitot tube, which may be protected on the ground with a removable pitot cover. It is important not to blow into either pitot or static vents; doing so can result in damage to the pressure instruments.

The left fuselage static vent.

The Heating and Ventilation System

Cabin heating is supplied by a shroud around the engine exhaust system. This allows air from inside the cowling to be warmed by the exhaust pipes. It can then be directed to outlets in the footwells (cabin heat) or at the lower windscreen (defrost) by two levers mounted on the lower left instrument panel. The system is very effective once the engine is warm, although its use is governed by a couple of safety factors.

First, the heating system effectively opens a path through the firewall between the engine compartment and the cockpit. For this reason, the cabin heat and defrost are selected OFF before engine start, or if fire is suspected in the engine compartment.

Second, with a system of this type there is a danger of carbon monoxide (CO) being introduced into the cabin. Carbon monoxide is a gas produced as a by-product of the combustion process. It is colorless, odorless and tasteless, but its effects are potentially fatal. A generally accepted practice is to shut off the heating system if engine fumes (which may contain CO) are thought to be entering the cockpit. The danger arises when a crack or split is present in the exhaust system inside the heating shroud, allowing carbon monoxide to enter the heating system.

The ventilation system consists of two cockpit vents, to the extreme right and left of the instrument panel, which control fresh air from their respective external air intakes located in the forward fuselage sides. The cockpit vents can be adjusted to control the direction and force of the fresh air into the cockpit. When the heating system is in use it is recommended that the fresh air vents be operated to give a comfortable temperature mix. Doing so will help to combat the possible danger of carbon monoxide poisoning, and will prevent the cabin from becoming "stuffy" and possibly inducing drowsiness in the pilot.

External air vent.

Seats and Harnesses

The seats are adjustable fore and aft. The handle which unlocks the seat position is located on the center of the seat frame below the forward edge of the seat cushion. This handle is raised (by turning 1/4 turn) and then the seat can be moved fore and aft. A recess is provided in the upper part of the instrument coaming in front of each pilot to give the necessary grip for the free hand. The control column, engine levers or coaming overhang should *not* be used as an alternative handgrip. The seat tracks are inclined so that as the seat is moved forward, the seating level is raised, and vice versa. When the desired position is reached, the handle is returned to the vertical position, and the pilot should check that the seat is positively locked in position. Generally, entry to and exit from the seats is easiest with the seats in the rearmost position. When the seats are unoccupied, the seat backs can be tilted forward to allow access to the baggage compartment.

Harness design may vary between different aircraft. In addition to the lap strap, shoulder straps of some description should be installed and their use should be considered mandatory; upper torso restraint has been shown to be a major factor in accident survivability. Final adjustment of the harness should be done when the seat is in the desired location.

The baggage area behind the seats is fitted with diagonal restraint straps for the securing of items placed in this area. Maximum baggage to be carried in this area is 100 lbs, evenly distributed so loading is not more than 25 lbs per square foot. Attention should be drawn to the weight and balance implications of weight in this area. Remember that for some maneuvers, carrying baggage is prohibited.

Doors and Windows

The Tomahawk has a door each side of the cabin to allow for easy access to the cabin by the wing walkways. These doors are fitted with two internal latches; the main door latch is located on the lower window sill. To lock this latch, the lever is moved forward to the horizontal position; to unlatch, the lever is moved up and back to slightly past the vertical position. There is also an upper latch to hold the top edge of each door securely to the airframe. Unfortunately, this latch is not as simple, or positive, in operation as the main latch. The lever must first be rotated to point forward, then rotated clockwise to point aft; during this rotation, the two top door hooks should engage on a loop in each door top. Operation of this upper latch is characterized by the force needed to bring the lever to the aft-pointing position. If the lever appears very slack in rotating, chances are that the doors have not latched. It is also possible that one door may latch, and not the other. Frequently, the plastic trim around the upper latch has been removed by operators to check door engagement, and to facilitate door latching.

Although it is important for the doors to be properly latched for flight, the consequences of partial door opening in flight are usually not serious. Where accidents do occur after a door opens in flight, they are often caused by pilot distraction, rather than as a direct result of the open door.

The roof-mounted door-locking handle.

When entering and leaving the cabin, the top of the doors should not be used as a hand grip to support body weight, because damage to the door and door hinges may result.

The door lever and storm (DV) window.

An inward opening STORM (DV) WINDOW is installed in the left-hand window. This window can be opened in flight when visibility through the windscreen has been impaired, or to aid ventilation.

The aircraft design and window area gives the Tomahawk exceptionally good all-round visibility. However, this visibility can be degraded by oil smears, insects and other matter accumulating on the windows. For window cleaning, a soft cloth and warm soapy water is recommended; to remove oil and grease, a cloth soaked in kerosene can be used. The use of gasoline, alcohol, thinners and window cleaner sprays is not recommended.

Section 2
Limitations

PA-38 Tomahawk A Pilot's Guide

PA-38 Tomahawk Dimensions

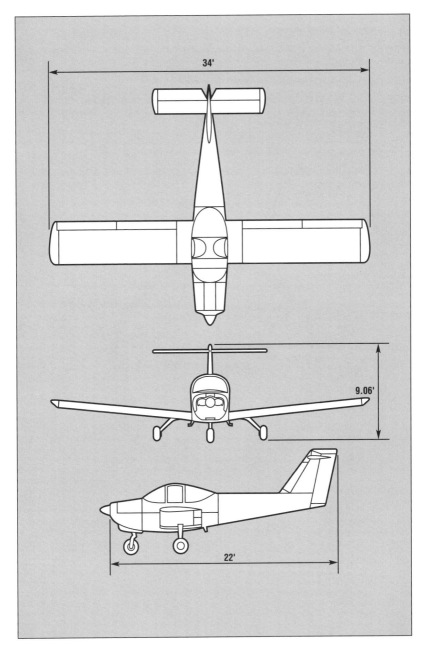

The "V" Airspeed Code

V_{S0} – (Low end of white arc) Stalling speed with full flaps.

V_{S1} – (Low end of green arc) Stalling speed without flaps.

V_{FE} – (Top of white arc) Maximum airspeed with flaps extended. Do not extend flaps above this speed, or fly faster than this speed with any flaps extended.

V_A – Design maneuvering speed. Do not make full or abrupt control movements when flying faster than this speed. Design maneuvering speed should not be exceeded when flying in turbulent conditions.

V_{NO} – (Top of green arc) Maximum structural cruising speed. Do not exceed this speed except in smooth air conditions.

V_{NE} – (Red line) Never exceed speed. Do not exceed this airspeed under any circumstances.

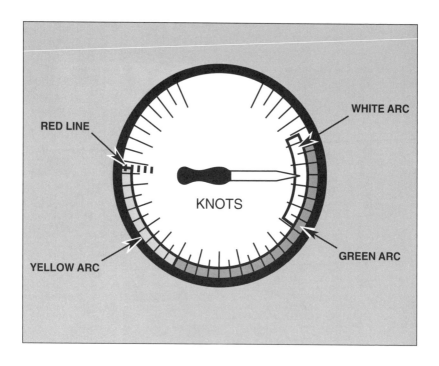

PA-38 Limitations

Airspeed Limitations

(quoted speeds are INDICATED airspeed—IAS)

	Knots	MPH
V_{NE}	138	159
V_{NO}	110	126
V_A (at 1,670 lbs)	103	118
V_A (at 1,277 lbs)	90	103
V_{FE}	89	102
Stalling Speed clean (with outboard flow strips only)	48	55
Stalling Speed clean (with inboard and outboard strips)	52	60
Stalling Speed Full Flaps (with outboard flow strips only)	47	54
Stalling Speed Full Flaps (with inboard and outboard strips)	49	56

Airspeed Indicator Markings

	Knots	MPH
RED LINE (Never Exceed)	138	159
YELLOW ARC (Caution range)	110 – 138	126 – 159
GREEN ARC (Normal operating range) —outboard flow strips	48 – 110	55 – 126
GREEN ARC (Normal operating range) —outboard and inboard strips	52 – 110	60 – 126
WHITE ARC (Flaps extended range) —outboard flow strips	47 – 89	54 – 102
WHITE ARC (Flaps extended range) —outboard and inboard strips	49 – 89	56 – 102

Maximum Demonstrated Crosswind Component

15 Knots

Airframe Limitations

Weights

	Normal	Utility
Maximum Takeoff Weight	1670 lbs	1670 lbs
Maximum Landing Weight	1670 lbs	1670 lbs
Maximum Baggage Weight	100 lbs	0

Flight Load Factors

Max. Positive load factor:	Normal	Utility
FLAPS UP	3.8G	4.4G
FLAPS DOWN	2.0G	2.0G

Max. Negative load factor: *No Inverted Maneuvers Permitted*

Performance Limitations

Service Ceiling	12,000 feet
Absolute Ceiling	14,000 feet

Engine Limitations

Maximum RPM	2,600

Oil System Limitations

	Oil Temperature	Instrument Marking
Normal operating range	75° – 245°F	Green Arc
Maximum	245°F	Red Line

	Oil Pressure	Instrument Marking
Normal operating range	60 – 90 psi	Green Arc
Minimum	15 psi	Red Line
Maximum	100 psi	Red Line
Caution range—idle	15 – 60 psi	Yellow Arc
Caution range—warm up	90 – 100 psi	Yellow Arc

Oil Quantity

	US Quart
Capacity	6
Minimum safe quantity	2 (+1 per hour planned flight)

Fuel System

Fuel Quantity	**US Gal**
Capacity	32
Unusable Fuel	2
Usable Fuel	30

Fuel Pressure		**Gauge Indication**
Maximum	8.0 psi	Red Line
Minimum	0.5 psi	Red Line
Normal operating range	0.5 – 8.0 psi	Green Arc

Miscellaneous Limitations

Tomahawk I

Nose Wheel Tire Pressure	26 psi	5.00 X 5
Main Wheel Tire Pressure	26 psi	5.00 X 5

Tomahawk II

Nose Wheel Tire Pressure	30 psi	6.00 X 6
Main Wheel Tire Pressure	30 psi	6.00 X 6

Oil Grades

Lycoming approves lubricating oil for the engine that conforms to specification MIL-L-6082 (straight mineral type) and specification MIL-L-22851 (ashless dispersant type).

Straight mineral oil is usually used only when the engine is new, or after maintenance work on the engine. Straight oil grades are known by their weight.

Ashless dispersant oils are more commonly used in service. Ashless dispersant type oil must not be used when the engine is operating on straight oil. It is therefore very important to check which type of oil is currently being used in the engine, and be sure only to add the same type.

Both types of oil are available in different grades, used according to the average surface air temperature. The recommended grades are set out as SAE numbers. The table below shows the recommended grades for various temperature bands.

AVERAGE SURFACE AIR TEMPERATURE	MIL-L-6082 Straight mineral
Above 60°F/16°C	SAE 50
30°F/-1°C – 90°F/32°C	SAE 40
0°F/-18°C – 70°F/21°C	SAE 30
Below 10°F/-12°C	SAE 20
AVERAGE SURFACE AIR TEMPERATURE	**MIL-L-22851 Ashless Dispersant**
Above 60°F/16°C	SAE 50 or SAE 40
30°F/-1°C – 90°F/32°C	SAE 40
0°F/-18°C – 70°F/21°C	SAE 30 or SAE 40
Below 10°F/-12°C	SAE 30

Fuel Grades

The PA-38 Tomahawk is certified for use with 100 LL fuels.

The table below shows the recommended fuel grades. It is wise to pay attention when your aircraft is being refueled, especially if at an airfield new to you. More than one pilot has found out that piston engines designed for AVGAS do not run very well on turbine fuel (Jet A-1). To help guard against this eventuality, AVGAS fueling points carry a RED sticker, and turbine fueling points a BLACK sticker.

APPROVED FUEL GRADES
100LL
100L
100

Section 3
Handling the Piper
PA-38 Tomahawk

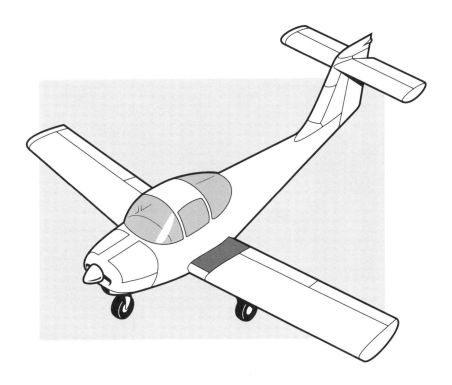

Engine Starting

Starting the Tomahawk is straightforward, but the ambient conditions and engine temperature are the prime factors to be considered. A cold engine

will require between 2 and 4 primes, a hot engine should not require any priming at all. The throttle is set to one quarter open (that is, 1/4-inch in), with the mixture rich and fuel set to the tank with the lowest quantity (unless, of course, that tank is empty). The Tomahawk is *not* fitted with an accelerator pump, and so "pumping" the throttle during starting will serve no purpose (other than to cause an excessively lean mixture).

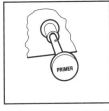

Cranking the starter should be limited to 30 seconds at a time due to the danger of the starter motor overheating. After a prolonged period of engine cranking without a successful start the starter should be allowed a few minutes to cool before a further attempt is made. The starter should not be operated after engine start, as damage to the starter may result.

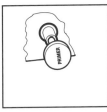

After start, the oil pressure should register within 30 seconds. Should the oil pressure not register, the engine should be shut down without delay. Readings on the suction gauge and ammeter are also usually checked after engine start.

Starting With a Suspected Flooded Engine

An over-primed (flooded) engine will be indicated by weak intermittent firing, and puffs of black smoke from the exhaust during the attempted start. If it is suspected that the engine is over-primed the throttle should be opened fully and the mixture moved to idle cut-off. If the engine starts, the throttle should be retarded to the normal position and the mixture moved to full rich.

Starting In Cold Ambient Conditions (below 0°C)

Failure to start due to an under-primed engine is more likely to occur in cold conditions with a cold engine. An under-primed engine will not fire at all, and additional priming is necessary. Starting in cold temperatures will be more difficult due to a number of factors. The oil will be more viscous, the battery may lose up to half of its capacity, and the fuel will not vaporize readily. A greater number of primes will be required, external power may be needed to supplement the aircraft battery, and pre-heat may be necessary in very low temperatures.

Taxiing

In the first few feet of taxiing, a brake check is normally carried out, followed by steering and differential brake checks in due course. It is common practice to check the hand-operated brake lever, in addition to the toe brakes. The direct link, via steering rods, from the rudder pedals to the nose wheel makes the Tomahawk easy to steer accurately. Use of differential brakes can give a very small turning circle, so increased power is often required when using prolonged differential braking. When taxiing with a crosswind "opposite rudder" will be required, up to full deflection. That is, with a crosswind from the left, up to full right rudder may be required as the aircraft tries to "weathervane" into the wind. In this situation, differential braking may also be required.

The chart below shows recommended control column positions when taxiing with the prevailing wind from the directions shown.

Speed control is important, especially when taxiing over rough surfaces or in strong wind conditions. When slowing the aircraft the throttle should always be closed first, and then the brakes evenly applied.

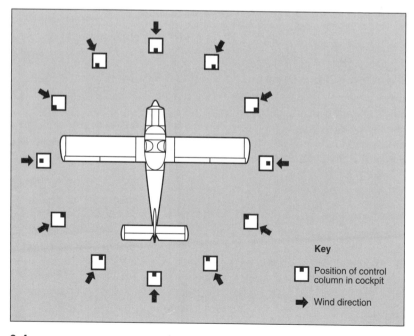

Key

⬛ Position of control column in cockpit

➡ Wind direction

Power and Pre-Takeoff Checks

The aircraft is usually positioned into the wind to aid engine cooling, and before the power checks start, the oil temperature should be in the green arc.

The engine is generally run up to 1,800-2,000 RPM, with the fuel tank with the greatest quantity selected (the same tank should be used for takeoff). At this RPM the carburetor heat is checked, and a small drop in RPM should be noted. An important point to note is that the inlet for the "hot" air is unfiltered, and so dust, grass, etc. may well enter the engine when "hot" air is selected, leading to increased engine wear. For this reason, the use of carburetor heat should be kept to the minimum necessary while on the ground. (*See* Section 4, Mixture and Carburetor Icing Supplement.)

The magnetos are checked individually, with no more than 3 seconds on each magneto being recommended to avoid spark plug fouling. A small drop in RPM is the norm and shows that the ignition system is functioning properly. No RPM drop at all when operating on one magneto may well indicate a malfunction in the ignition system, and the possibility that one or both magnetos are staying "live." An excessive drop in RPM when operating on one magneto, especially when accompanied by rough running, may indicate fouled spark plugs or a faulty magneto. If fouled plugs are suspected it may be possible to clear the problem. The engine is set to about 2,000 RPM with magnetos on BOTH, and the mixture leaned to give the "peak" RPM. This should be held for about 10 seconds, then the mixture returned to full rich, and the magnetos re-checked.

> **WARNING:** Excessive power setting and over-lean mixture settings should be avoided during this procedure. If the problem does not clear, the aircraft should be considered unserviceable.

The engine gauges, together with the suction gauge and ammeter, are checked at 1,800-2,000 RPM for normal indications.

Takeoff

Normally, takeoff is made with the mixture in the full RICH position. At high elevation airfields (above 3,000 feet MSL) it may be necessary to lean the mixture before takeoff to give maximum power.

For all takeoffs, care must be taken to ensure that the feet remain clear of the toe brakes; this is best done by keeping the heels on the floor. Inadvertent pressure on the toe brakes can significantly slow the aircraft during the takeoff run, and lead to directional control difficulties.

At the start of the takeoff run (as at all other times), the throttle should be opened smoothly and progressively; rapid opening of the throttle should be specifically avoided. The normal rotation speed is 53 knots, with a climb speed of 70 knots dependent on conditions and operator procedures. In crosswind conditions, the Tomahawk can prove to be a handful, particularly in directional control as the speed increases prior to rotation. The recommended rotation speed in a crosswind is 60 knots. For "short field" takeoffs, the use of one stage of flaps (21°) is common practice.

On rough surfaces particularly, it is important to protect the nose wheel by keeping weight off of it during the takeoff run; although "over-rotating" should be avoided as this will lengthen the takeoff run—and ruin the view ahead!

Climbing

An airspeed in the region of 70 knots will give the best rate of climb after takeoff. The best angle of climb (the best increase in height for the shortest distance traveled over the ground) is obtained at 61 knots when one stage of flaps is lowered. While climbing it is important to monitor the engine gauges, as the engine is operating at a high power setting but with a reduced cooling airflow compared to cruising flight. Lookout ahead is impaired by the high nose attitude, and it is good airmanship to "weave" the nose periodically during the climb to visually check the area ahead.

Cruising Flight

Cruising is normally done with a power setting of 55 – 75%. Typically, a setting of about 2,200 RPM will give an indicated airspeed of around 90 knots.

Engine Handling

Engine rough-running can be caused by a number of factors. Unfortunately, the majority of engine failures in light aircraft are caused by pilot error. After carburetor icing, fuel exhaustion (running out of fuel) or fuel starvation (i.e., fuel on-board but not reaching the engine) are common causes of engine failure. Having sufficient fuel on board to complete the flight is a point of basic airmanship, and can be accomplished by proper flight planning and thorough pre-flight checks. In flight, keeping the fuel tanks in balance and monitoring the fuel system are a function of the cruise checks. In the Tomahawk, fuel starvation may occur if the engine-driven fuel pump fails. In this instance, the use of the electric fuel pump should restore the fuel supply to the engine and allow for a diversion to be made.

Regular monitoring of the engine instruments may forewarn of an impending problem. HIGH OIL TEMPERATURE may indicate a faulty gauge, if not accompanied by a corresponding drop in oil pressure. The action taken will depend on the pilot's judgment of the situation at the time. A reasonable course of action would be a diversion to a suitable airfield, while remaining alert to the possibility of a sudden engine failure. *Where high oil temperature is accompanied by a low oil pressure, engine failure may very well be imminent, and the pilot should act accordingly.* Such a situation might occur during a prolonged slow climb in hot conditions. In this instance, increasing the airspeed to provide more cooling, and reducing power, if possible, may restore oil temperature to normal. In the event of a LOW OIL PRESSURE reading, accompanied by a normal oil temperature reading, gauge failure may be the culprit, and the pilot can consider actions similar to those for an oil temperature gauge failure.

Stalling

A Reminder: The information in this section is no substitute for flight instruction under the guidance of a flight instructor familiar with the aircraft and its characteristics.

The Tomahawk is conventional in its stalling behavior. The stall warning horn activates at 5 to 10 knots above the stall airspeed. Because this horn is electrically operated, the stall warning system is inoperative with the master switch off, or with a faulty electrical system. The actual stall speed can be affected by many factors including the aircraft weight and center of gravity position. The use of power will lower the stalling speed, while turning flight raises the stall speed. The use of flaps, power or turning flight considerably increases the chances of a wing drop at the stall. When practicing stalls, the possibility of a wing drop can be reduced by keeping the aircraft coordinated during the approach to the stall. Typical height loss for a full stall with a conventional recovery (using power) is about 200 feet. Airframe buffeting (mostly of the tail surfaces) precedes the stall and is a feature of the Tomahawk.

There is a 1-knot differential between zero flap (V_{S1}) and full flap stalling speeds (V_{S0}), for models with outboard flow strips only, which gives a good indication of the overall lack of effectiveness of the flaps.

Stalling in the Tomahawk is usually achieved with the control wheel held fully aft. There have been instances where in this position, the control shaft has been lifted vertically, binding the control wheel and preventing any forward movement. A modification is available to prevent this happening; however, care should be taken when the control wheel is being held fully aft.

Spins

A Reminder: The information in this section is no substitute for flight instruction under the guidance of a flight instructor familiar with the aircraft and its characteristics.

The Tomahawk is approved for intentional spinning when operating in the utility category; however,

INTENTIONAL SPINS WITH FLAPS EXTENDED ARE PROHIBITED.

The Tomahawk spin has been the center of much comment and discussion since the aircraft entered service. This may be because it does exhibit what can be described as "classic" spin and spin recovery characteristics, which perhaps are not so apparent on other contemporary training aircraft.

As with stalling, several factors can effect the behavior of the aircraft in the spin. It is possible to devote a whole book just to this subject, and it is not the intention here to write a textbook on spinning. However, some points are worthy of mention. The weight of the aircraft (and particularly the CG position) has a noticeable effect on the spin. High weights tend to extend the spin recovery, due to the increase in inertia. The position of the ailerons is important in spinning. The ailerons should be held NEUTRAL throughout the spin and recovery.

Piper recommends that the aircraft should be trimmed for a glide at 75 knots, and that the spin is entered power off at the stall. The spin is fairly standard; it is the spin recovery that must be carefully considered. As normal full rudder is applied opposite to the spin direction, the control wheel is moved rapidly forward **without delay**. You should note that in the Tomahawk, the control wheel will probably need to be *fully forward* (in other words, full down elevator) to achieve spin recovery. The immediate result may be that the spin steepens and speeds up. This sometimes leads the pilot to think that incorrect actions have been taken—this is not the case. There is usually a delay of between 1/2 and 1-1/2 turns before the spin stops, during this time the full and proper recovery actions must be maintained. The recovery occurs with a steep nose down attitude; for this reason, it is acceptable to relax the forward pressure on the control wheel *once the aircraft has stopped spinning*. The rudder is then centered, and the aircraft is recovered from the dive. Due to the steep nose down attitude in the recovery, it is important to quickly center the rudder before the speed builds up above V_A (103 knots). The dive out following spin recovery is characterized by the high speed reached and height lost.

To summarize, the spin recovery is as follows:

- Check ailerons neutral and throttle closed.

- Apply and maintain full opposite rudder (opposite to the direction of spin).

- Move the control wheel immediately forward and maintain until the stall is broken and the spin stops. When the spin stops, it is permissible to relax the forward pressure on the control wheel to reduce the nose down attitude in the dive out.

- When spin stops center the rudder quickly, and recover from the ensuing dive.

Descent

The descent may be powered or glide. For the glide, a speed of 70 knots is standard. Where flaps are used the rate of descent increases, the initial lowering of flaps leads to a slight nose down pitching and reduced airspeed. The low power settings usually used during the descent, and a possible prolonged descent into warmer air, provide ideal conditions for carburetor icing. Full carburetor heat should be used where necessary, and in a glide descent power should be added for short periods throughout the descent to help prevent plug fouling, rapid cylinder cooling, and of course, carburetor icing.

Landing

For the approach to landing, the mixture should be full RICH (unless landing at a very high elevation airfield), the electric fuel pump should be on and the fuel tank with the most fuel selected. The Tomahawk is almost universally described as being an easy aircraft to land, the elevator being particularly effective right through the landing. This does not prevent the Tomahawk (as with many other light aircraft) appearing year after year in landing accident reports. It is rare that anybody is hurt in these accidents, but the reports seem surprisingly similar:

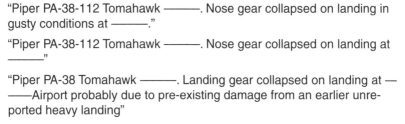

"Piper PA-38-112 Tomahawk ———. Nose gear collapsed on landing in gusty conditions at ———."

"Piper PA-38-112 Tomahawk ———. Nose gear collapsed on landing at ———"

"Piper PA-38 Tomahawk ———. Landing gear collapsed on landing at ———Airport probably due to pre-existing damage from an earlier unreported heavy landing"

The nose wheel is not nearly as strong as the main landing gear, but there is no need for its strength to be tested if a proper approach and landing technique is used. Approach speed for a normal approach with flaps is about 70 knots, and usually a little higher for a flapless approach.

Incorrect approach speed is a primary cause of "ballooning," which often leads to bouncing. Bouncing also occurs where the aircraft is allowed to touch down at too high a speed, usually in a level attitude rather than a nose-up attitude. The correct action in either a "balloon" or a bounce is to GO AROUND without delay. The correct landing technique is to approach at the proper speed, "flare" or "hold off," close the throttle, and gradually raise the nose to ensure a slow touchdown speed *on the mainwheels first,* with the nose wheel still off the ground. With the effectiveness of the Tomahawk elevators this should be no problem. As the aircraft slows down, correct use of the elevators means the nose wheel is allowed to gently contact the surface sometime after the initial mainwheel contact. Again, there is no substitute for flight instruction in the proper technique with a flight instructor.

The go-around in the Tomahawk does not provide any problems, even with full flaps extended. The trim change when applying full power is manageable, and although the aircraft will climb with full flaps extended, it is common practice to raise flaps to the first stage (21°) as part of the go-around procedure.

Parking and Tie Down

The aircraft is generally parked into the wind; it is good practice to stop with the nose wheel straight so that the rudder is not deflected. All switches should be off, and the doors closed. In extremely cold weather it may be advisable *not* to set the parking brake as moisture may freeze the brakes. Also, the parking brake should not be set if there is reason to believe that the brakes are overheated. If for any reason the parking brake is not set, the wheels should be "chocked."

When tying down the aircraft, the following technique is recommended:

- Park the aircraft into the wind with the flaps retracted.
- Secure the flight controls by looping the seat belt through the control wheel.
- Tie ropes, cables or chains are attached to the wing tie-down points and secured to ground anchor points.
- If desired, a rope (not cable or chain) can be secured to the nose gear and secured to a ground anchor point.
- A rope can be passed through the tail tie-down point and each end secured at a 45° angle each side of the tail.
- External control locks may be advisable in strong or gusty wind conditions.

It is also prudent to use a pitot cover, particularly if the aircraft will be left unattended for some time.

Good tie down can prevent wind damage!

Section 4
Mixture and Carburetor Icing Supplement

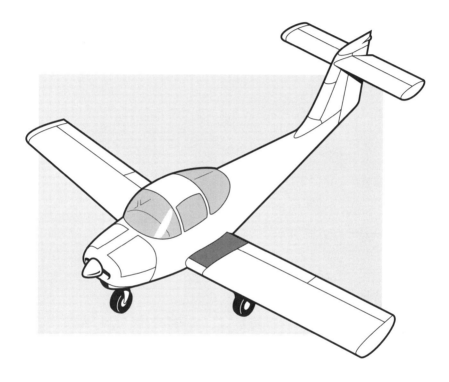

Carburetor Icing

Almost certainly the most common cause of engine rough-running, and complete engine failure, is carburetor icing. Despite this, carburetor icing remains a widely misunderstood subject. Many pilots' knowledge of the subject is limited to a feeling that the carburetor heat should be used regularly in flight, without really knowing the symptoms of carburetor icing or the conditions most likely to cause its formation.

How Carburetor Icing Forms

IMPACT ICING occurs when ice forms over the external air inlet (air filter) and inside the induction system leading to the carburetor. This type of icing occurs with the temperature below 0°C while flying in clouds, or in precipitation (i.e., rain, sleet or snow). These conditions are also conducive to airframe icing, and the aircraft is *not cleared for flight into known icing conditions,* which clearly these are. So, assuming the aircraft is operated legally within its limitations, this form of icing should not occur, and is not considered further.

CARBURETOR ICING is caused by a temperature drop inside the carburetor, which can happen even in conditions where other forms of icing will not occur. The causes of this temperature drop are twofold:

1. FUEL ICING—the evaporation of fuel inside the carburetor. Liquid fuel changes to fuel vapor and mixes with the induction air causing a large temperature drop. If the temperature inside the carburetor falls below 0°C, water vapor in the atmosphere condenses into ice, usually on the walls of the carburetor passage adjacent to the fuel jet, and on the throttle valve. Generally, fuel icing is responsible for around 70% of the temperature drop in the carburetor.

2. THROTTLE ICING—the temperature loss caused by the acceleration of air and consequent pressure drop around the throttle valve. This effect may again take the temperature below 0°C, and water vapor in the inlet air will condense into ice on the throttle valve. This practical effect is a demonstration of Bernoulli's Principle.

As fuel and throttle icing generally occur together, they are known just as carburetor icing.

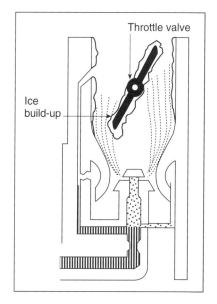

Throttle valve

Ice build-up

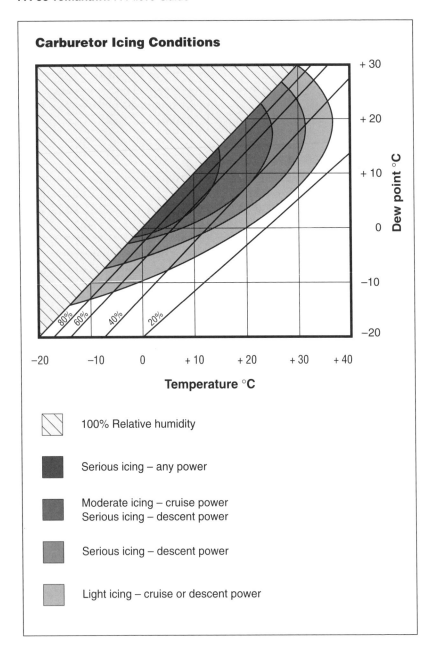

Conditions Likely to Lead to Carburetor Icing

Two criteria govern the likelihood of carburetor icing conditions: the AIR TEMPERATURE and the RELATIVE HUMIDITY.

The ambient air temperature is important, *but not because the temperature needs to be below 0°C, or even close to freezing.* The temperature drop in the carburetor can be up to 30°C, so carburetor icing can (and does) occur in hot ambient conditions. It is no wonder carburetor icing is sometimes referred to as refrigeration icing. Carburetor icing is considered a possibility within the temperature range of -10°C to +30°C.

The relative humidity (a measure of the water content of the atmosphere) is a major factor. The greater the water content in the atmosphere (the higher the relative humidity), the greater the risk of carburetor icing. That said, the relative humidity (RH) does not to have to be 100% (i.e., visible water droplets—cloud, rain), for carburetor icing to occur. Carburetor icing is considered a possibility at relative humidity values as low as 30%. Herein lies perhaps the real danger of carburetor icing, that it can occur in such a wide range of conditions. Obviously the pilot must be alert to the possibility of carburetor icing at just about all times. Flight in or near clouds, or in other visible moisture (i.e., rain) might be an obvious cause of carburetor icing, but—*visible moisture does not need to be present for carburetor icing to occur.*

Symptoms of Carburetor Icing

In this aircraft, fitted with a fixed pitch propeller, the symptoms of carburetor icing are straightforward. A loss of RPM will be the first symptom, although this is often first noticed as a loss of altitude. As the icing becomes more serious, engine rough-running may occur.

Carburetor icing is often detected during the use of the carburetor heat. Normally when the carburetor heat is used, a small drop in RPM occurs; when the control is returned to cold (off) the RPM restores to the same as before the use of carburetor heat. If the RPM restores to a figure higher than before the carburetor heat was used, it can be assumed that some form of carburetor icing was present.

Use of Carburetor Heat

Apart from the normal check of carburetor heat during the power checks, it may be necessary to use the carburetor heat on the ground if carburetor icing is suspected. Safety considerations apart, the use of carburetor heat on the ground should be kept to a minimum, because the hot air inlet is unfiltered and sand or dust can enter the engine, increasing engine wear.

Carburetor icing is generally considered to be very unlikely with the engine operating at above 75% power, i.e., during the takeoff and climb. Carburetor heat should not be used with the engine operating at above 75% power (i.e., full throttle) as detonation may occur. Detonation is the uncontrolled burning of fuel in the cylinders, literally an explosion, and will cause serious damage to the engine very quickly. Apart from the danger of detonation, the use of carburetor heat reduces the power the engine produces. In any situation where full power is required (i.e., takeoff, climb, go-around) the carburetor heat must be off (cold).

Very few operators recommend the use of anything other than FULL carburetor heat. A normal carburetor icing check will involve leaving the carburetor heat on (hot) for 5 to 10 seconds, although the pilot may wish to vary this dependent on the conditions. The use of carburetor heat does increase the fuel consumption, and this may be a factor to consider if the aircraft is being flown towards the limit of its range/endurance in possible carburetor icing conditions.

With carburetor icing present, the use of carburetor heat may lead to a large drop in RPM, with rough running. The instinctive reaction is to put the carburetor heat back to cold (off), and quickly—this is, however, the wrong action. Chances are this rough running is a good thing, and the carburetor heat should be left on (hot) until the rough running clears, and the RPM rises. In this instance, the use of carburetor heat has melted a large amount of accumulated icing, and the melted ice is passing through the engine causing temporary rough running.

Care should be taken when flying in very cold ambient conditions (below -10°C). In these conditions the use of carburetor heat may actually raise

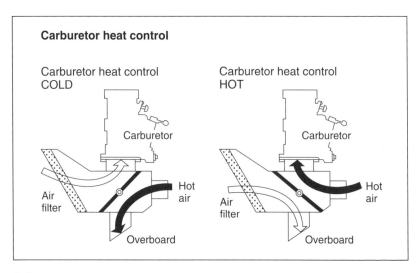

Carburetor heat control

Carburetor heat control
COLD

Carburetor

Air filter

Hot air

Overboard

Carburetor heat control
HOT

Carburetor

Air filter

Hot air

Overboard

the temperature in the carburetor to that most conducive to carburetor icing. Generally, when the temperature in the carburetor is below -8°C, moisture forms directly into ice crystals which pass through the engine.

The RPM loss normally associated with the use of carburetor heat is caused by the reduced density of the hot air entering the carburetor, leading to an over-rich mixture entering the engine. If the carburetor heat has to be left constantly on (hot)—i.e., flight in heavy rain and clouds—it may be advisable to lean the mixture in order to maintain RPM and smooth engine running.

It is during the descent (and particularly the glide descent) that carburetor icing is most likely to occur. The position of the throttle valve (i.e., almost closed) is a contributory factor, and even though the carburetor heat is normally applied throughout a glide descent, the low engine power will reduce the temperature of the hot air selected with the carburetor heat control. In addition, a loss of power may not be readily noticed, as the propeller is likely to windmill even after a complete loss of power. A full loss of power may only be apparent when the throttle is opened at the bottom of the descent. This is one good reason for opening the throttle to "clear the engine" at intervals during a glide descent.

The Mixture Control

The aircraft is provided with a mixture control, so that the pilot can adjust the fuel/air mixture entering the engine when necessary. The cockpit mixture control operates a needle valve between the float bowl and the main metering jet. This valve controls the fuel flow to the main metering jet to adjust the mixture. With the mixture control in the idle cut-off position (full lean), the valve is fully closed.

Reasons for Adjusting the Mixture

Correct leaning of the engine will enable the engine to be operated at its most efficient in terms of fuel consumption. With the increased use of 100LL fuel, leaning is also important to reduce spark plug fouling.

The most efficient engine operation is obtained with a fuel/air ratio of about 1:15; that is, 1 part fuel to 15 parts air. In fact, with the mixture set to full rich, the system is designed to give a slightly richer mixture than ideal; typically about 1:12. This slightly over-rich mixture reduces the possibility of pre-ignition or detonation, and aids cylinder cooling.

Effects of Mixture Adjustment

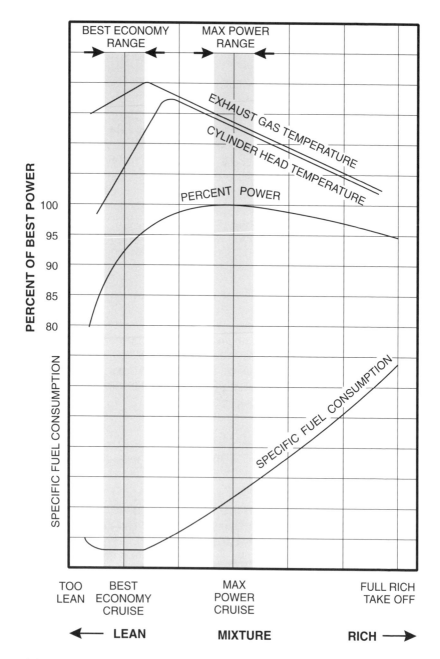

As altitude increases, the air density decreases. Above about 3,000 feet the reduced air density can lead to an over-rich mixture. If the mixture becomes excessively rich, power will be lost, rough running may be evident and ultimately engine failure will occur due to a "rich out." It is for this reason that the mixture control is provided to ensure the correct fuel/air ratio; typically it is used when cruising above 3,000 feet.

The flight manuals for some older aircraft recommend leaning only above 5,000 feet. However, with the increasing use of AVGAS 100LL, and the plug fouling problems sometimes associated with 100LL, most operators recommend leaning once above 3,000 feet.

Use of the Mixture Control

For takeoff and climb, the mixture should be full rich; the only exception is operation from a high density altitude airport, when leaning may be necessary to ensure the availability of maximum power. On reaching a cruising altitude above about 3,000 feet, the cruise power should be set, and then leaning can be carried out. (Note: Generally, leaning with over 75% power set is not recommended.) If climbing above about 5,000 feet, full throttle will be less than 75% power on a normally aspirated engine, and so leaning may be permissible to maintain smooth running.

Assuming that there is no Exhaust Gas Temperature (EGT) gauge and no cylinder head temperature gauge, the primary instrument to watch when leaning is the RPM gauge (tachometer).

To lean the engine, the recommended power setting (RPM) is set with the throttle. Next, with a constant throttle setting, the mixture control is slowly moved back (leaned). If leaning is required, the RPM will increase slowly, peak, and then decrease as the mixture is leaned. If leaning is continued, the engine will ultimately run rough and lose power.

If the mixture is set to achieve peak RPM, the maximum power mixture has been achieved.

If the mixture is set to give a tachometer reading 25 to 50 RPM less than peak RPM on the "lean" side, the best economy mixture has been achieved. This setting is the one that many aircraft manufacturers recommend, and their performance claims are based on such a procedure.

Using a mixture that is too lean is a false economy, and will lead to serious engine damage sooner or later. Detonation (an uncontrolled explosive combustion of the mixture in the cylinder) is particularly dangerous, and can lead to an engine failure in a very short time. The use of a full rich mixture during full power operations is specifically to ensure engine cooling and guard against detonation.

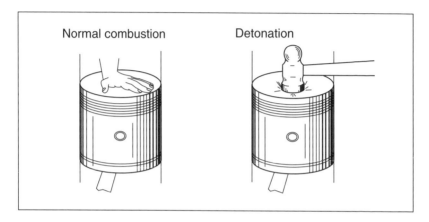

For any change in operating conditions (altitude, power setting) the mixture will need to be reset. It is particularly important that the mixture is set to full rich before increasing the power setting.

During a descent from a high altitude, the mixture will gradually become too lean if not enriched, leading to excessive cylinder temperatures, power loss and ultimately engine failure. Normally, the mixture is set to full rich prior to landing, unless operating at a high elevation airfield.

Moving the mixture to the full lean position—ICO (idle cut-off)—closes the needle valve, and so stops fuel supply to the main metering jet. This is the normal method for shutting down the engine and ensures that no unburned fuel mixture is left in the engine.

Section 5
Expanded PA-38
Pre-Flight Checklist

Approaching Aircraft

1. Check for and remove any tie-downs, external control locks, pitot cover and wheel chocks.

2. Look for any oil and fuel spillage from aircraft.

3. Remove any ice and frost from *all* surfaces.

4. Check for access to taxiways, obstructions, loose gravel, etc.

5. Look to see if aircraft is on a level surface. This may effect the visual check of fuel quantity.

In Cabin

1. **Internal Control locks and covers** .... Remove, stow securely.

2. **Parking Brake** .... Check ON with locking plate in.

3. **Magneto Switch** .... Check OFF and key out.

4. **Master Switch** .... On. Turn on pitot heater, anti-collision lights, landing light and navigation lights. Leave cockpit and check:

5. **Stall Warning Vane** .... Move gently forward to check for operation.

6. **Pitot Heat** .... Check with fingers that pitot tube is warm (it may take a minute or so to warm up)

7. **Anti-Collision Lights** .... Check operation. Do not look directly at strobes while they are operating.

8. **Landing/Nav lights** .... Check. The navigation lights colors are: PORT (Left) – red; STARBOARD (Right) – green; REAR (Tail) – white. Return to cockpit and turn off electrical services.

9. **Fuel Selector Valve** .... Turn on—Check quantity gauges.

10. **Master Switch** .... Off.

11. **Flaps** .... Lower to first stage (21°). Check for loose articles around the flap lever.

12. **Trim Wheel** .... Check position neutral using indicator.

13. **First Aid Kit** .... Check in position, secure.

14. **Fire Extinguisher** .... Check in position, secure and serviceable (gauge at top should be in green arc).

15. **Cockpit** .... Check for and remove/stow any loose articles.

External

Leave cockpit and begin at rear of wing. This should also be where you complete your checks.

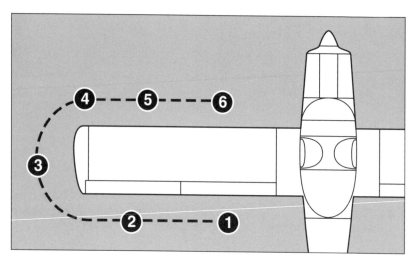

Port Wing

1. **Flap** .... Check upper and lower surface condition. Particularly check inner lower surface for caked mud or stone damage from wheels. Check linkages secure and greased.

2. **Aileron** .... Check upper and lower surface condition, linkages and hinges secure. With fingers inside hinge line, (hold the aileron with other hand), check balance weight is secure (next to wing tip). Check full and free movement— *do not use force.*

3. **Wing Tip** .... Check condition, security; Nav and strobe lights unbroken (This area is particularly vulnerable to hangar damage).

4. **Wing Surface** .... Check upper and lower surface condition.

5. **Wing Leading Edge** ....Check for dents along entire length. Check stall warning vane movement gently— a click should be heard. Check pitot tube perforations unblocked— *do not blow into pitot tube.*

6. **Fuel Tank** .... Check contents visually, resecure cap. Check fuel vent unblocked. Take fuel drain sample from under tank if necessary—check for correct color, water bubbles or sediment. Check drain not leaking.

Port Landing Gear

1. **Tire** .... Check for tread and general condition. Check for correct inflation. Check alignment of creep marks.

2. **Hydraulic Lines** .... Check for leaks (red fluid).

3. **Disc Brake** .... Should be shiny, not rusty or pitted.

4. **Strut and Fairing** .... Check condition, especially fiberglass fairing. Look for mud or stone damage on wing and flap surface near landing gear.

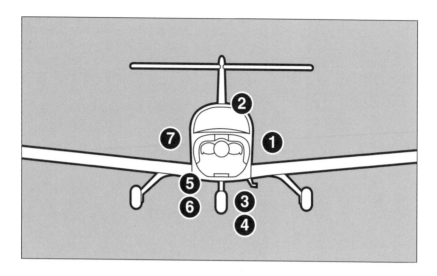

Front Fuselage and Engine

1. **Port Cowling** .... Open, check brake fluid level, and engine compartment generally (i.e., HT leads secure, oil leaks). Resecure cowling, take fuel sample if necessary. Check fuel drain not leaking.

2. **Windscreen** .... Should be clean and insect free, OAT probe secure.

3. **Nose Strut** .... Check oleo extension correct, linkages, nuts and split pins secure.

4. **Nose Wheel** .... Check for tread and general condition. Check for correct inflation. Check alignment of creep marks.

5. **Front Cowling** .... Check condition and security. Intakes clear, landing light unbroken.

6. **Propeller** .... Look for cracks or chips, especially leading edge. Check spinner secure and condition good. *Do not move or swing propeller.*

7. **Starboard Cowling** .... Open engine compartment, check oil level, *do not* overtighten dipstick on resecuring. Check engine compartment (i.e., HT leads secure etc.). Resecure cowling.

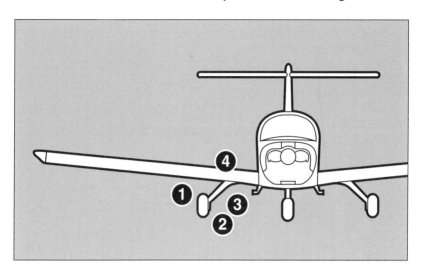

Starboard Landing Gear

1. **Tire** .... Check for tread and general condition. Check for correct inflation. Look for alignment of creep marks.

2. **Hydraulic Lines** .... Check for leaks (red fluid).

3. **Disc Brake** .... Should be shiny, not rusty or pitted.

4. **Strut and Fairing** .... Check condition, especially fiberglass fairing. Look for mud or stone damage on wing and flap surface near landing gear.

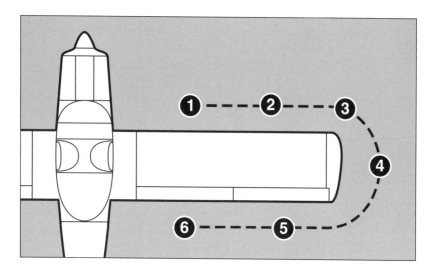

Starboard Wing

1. **Fuel Tank** .... Check quantity visually, resecure cap. Check fuel vent (under wing) unblocked. Take fuel drain sample. Check that drain is not leaking.

2. **Wing Leading Edge** .... Check for dents along entire length.

3. **Wing Surface** .... Check upper and lower surface condition.

4. **Wing Tip** .... Check condition, security; nav and strobe lights unbroken.

5. **Aileron** .... Check upper and lower surface condition, linkages and hinges secure, balance weight (next to wing tip) secure. Remember to watch for aileron movement while checking inside hinge line. Check full and free movement gently—*do not use force.*

6. **Flap** .... Check upper and lower surface condition, especially near landing gear. Check linkages secure and greased.

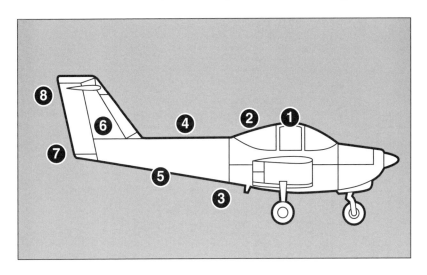

Starboard Fuselage

1. **Cockpit Door** .... Check latch and hinges secure.
2. **Windows** .... Check—clean and uncracked.
3. **Skin** .... Check general surface condition upper and lower, look for wrinkles, dents or punctures.
4. **Radio Antennas** .... Check secure.
5. **Static Vent** .... Check clear and unblocked *Do not blow into vent.*
6. **Tail Fin** .... Check skin condition, especially fairings. Check antennas secure.
7. **Rudder** .... Check condition, linkages secure and greased, nuts and split pins secure, nav light unbroken. *Do not attempt to force rudder movement.*
8. **Horizontal Stabilizer/Elevator** .... Check condition, linkages secure. Check other side of tail fin.

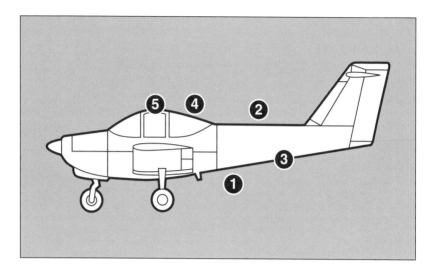

Port Fuselage

1. **Skin** .... Check general surface condition, upper and lower, look for any wrinkles, dents or punctures.

2. **Radio Antennas** .... Check secure.

3. **Static Vent** ...... Check clear and unblocked—*do not blow into vent.*

4. **Windows** .... Check clean and uncracked.

5. **Cockpit door** .... Check latches and hinges secure.

Important

Remember: Full reference must be made to airplane flight manual, Pilot's Operating Handbook, flight school syllabus, etc., for normal and emergency procedures.

If in doubt—ask

Section 6
Loading and Performance

Loading

Aircraft loading can divided into two areas, the aircraft weight and the center of gravity (CG) position.

The aircraft must be loaded so that its weight is below the certified maximum takeoff weight (1,670 lbs). The weight limit is set primarily as a function of the lifting capability of the aircraft, which is largely determined by the wing design and engine power of the aircraft. Operating the aircraft when it is over weight will adversely effect the aircraft handling and performance, such as:

> Increased takeoff speed and slower acceleration
>
> Increased runway length required for takeoff
>
> Reduced rate of climb
>
> Reduced maximum altitude capability
>
> Reduced range and endurance
>
> Reduction in maneuverability and controllability
>
> Increased stall speed
>
> Increased approach and landing speed
>
> Increased runway length required for landing

The aircraft must also be loaded to ensure that its center of gravity (CG) is within set limits, normally defined as a forward and aft limit in inches aft of the datum. For the Tomahawk, the datum is the tip of the spinner. The forward limit is determined by the amount of elevator control available at landing speed, the aft limit is determined by the stability and controllability of the aircraft while maneuvering. Attempted flight with the CG position outside of the set limits (either forward or aft) will lead to control difficulties, and possibly loss of control of the aircraft.

When loading the aircraft it is standard practice to calculate the weight and CG position of the aircraft at the same time, commonly known as the weight and balance calculation. Before going further it must be emphasized that the following examples are provided for illustrative purposes only. Each *individual* aircraft has an *individual* weight and balance record that is valid only for that aircraft, and is dependent among other things on the equipment installed in the aircraft. If the aircraft has any major modification, repair or new equipment installed, a new weight and balance record will be produced. Therefore, for any loading or performance calculations, you must use the documents for the specific aircraft you will be flying.

As well as setting out limits, the aircraft documents will also give arms for each item of loading. The arm is a distance from the aircraft datum to the item. The weight multiplied by its arm gives its moment. Thus a set weight will have a greater moment the further away it is from the datum.

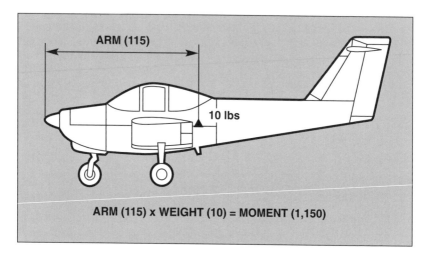

The operating weight of the aircraft can be split into two categories:

EMPTY WEIGHT—the weight of the aircraft, including unusable fuel; normally this includes full oil as well. The weight and CG position of the aircraft in this condition will be noted in the weight and balance record.

USEFUL LOAD —weight of a pilot, passenger, usable fuel and baggage.

Weight and Center of Gravity Record

Produced by:

Grosvenor Aviation Services (Engineering) Limited

Aircraft Type:

Piper PA-38-112

Nationality and Registration Marks:

N-BGRR

Constructor's Serial Number:

78A0336

Maximum Permissible Weight:

1670 lbs

Maximum Landing Weight:

1670 lbs

Center of Gravity Limits:

Refer to Flight Manual Rep No. FAA 2126

All arms are distances in inches either fore or aft of datum.

Part "A" Basic Weight

The basic weight of this aircraft as calculated from Planeweighs Limited Report No. 1034 weighed on 08.07.88. at Manchester Airport is: **1182 lbs**

The center of gravity of aircraft in the same condition (aft of the datum) is: **74.66 inches**

The total Moment about the datum in this condition in lb inches is: **88254.45**

The DATUM referred to is defined in the Flight Manual, which is **66.25 inches** forward of wing leading edge.

The basic weight includes the weight of 12 lbs unusable fuel and 45 lbs of oil and the weight of items indicated in Appendix 1 which comprises the list of basic equipment carried.

Each individual aircraft has an individual weight and balance record, valid only for that aircraft.

Mathematical Weight And Balance Calculation

With this method of calculation, the weights of each item are listed together with their arm. Addition of all the weights is the first step, to ensure that the resulting figure is within the maximum permitted. Assuming this is the case, the balance can then be calculated. For each item (except for the basic weight where the calculation is done already on the weight and balance record) the weight is multiplied by the arm, to give a moment. Normally the arm is aft of the datum, to give a positive figure. If the arm quoted is forward of the datum the moment will be negative (although obviously the weight is *not* deducted from the weight calculation). All the moments are then added together, to give the total moment, and this figure is then divided by the total weight. The resulting figure will be the position of the CG, which can be checked to ensure it is within the set limits. The weight and CG position can be plotted on a graph in the flight manual. If the plotted position is within the "envelope," the weight and CG position are within limits.

Example:

Empty Weight: N-1234
From the weight and balance record, weight is 1,182 lbs

Useful Load: Pilot 155 lbs
Passenger 140 lbs
Rear Baggage 10 lbs
Fuel Full (30 US Gallons) 180 lbs

You can simply add together the weights at this stage to check the total weight; however, it is more common to make up a table to check weight *and* balance. From the information above and on the weight and balance record, we know the weight and arm for each item. The table is used to calculate the moment for each item (i.e., the weight x the arm).

ITEM	WEIGHT (lbs)	ARM	MOMENT
Empty Weight: the weight, arm and moment are listed in the weight and balance record.			
Aircraft N-1234	1,182	74.66	88,248.10
Useful Load			
Pilot	155	85.5	13,252.50
Passenger	140	85.5	11,970.00
Rear Baggage	10	115.0	1,150.00
Fuel	180	75.4	13,572.00
Total Weight	1,667	Total Moment	128,192.60

Total weight, at 1,667 lbs, is below the maximum permitted and so is acceptable.

To find the Center of Gravity position, the total moment is divided by the total weight:

$$\frac{128,192.60}{1,667} = 76.90 \text{ (inches aft of datum)}$$

This weight and center of gravity position can now be plotted on the Weight and Center of Gravity Envelope in the flight manual to check if it is within limits.

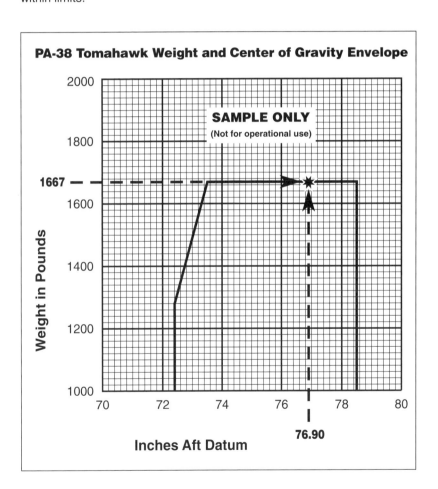

Use of the Loading Graph

One problem with the mathematical calculation of weight and balance is the amount of math involved—especially if you don't have a calculator handy!

The loading graph can help here by cutting out the math needed to calculate the moment. On the loading graph, the mathematics of multiplying the weight by the arm is done for you (you don't even need to know the arm).

Using the same figures as before we can get the moments for the variable and disposable loads from the loading graph:

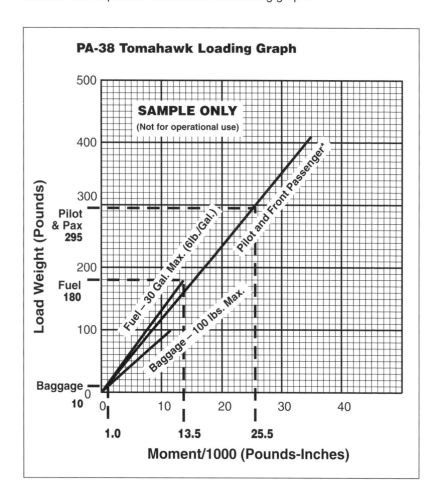

Now we can put these figures into a simplified table:

ITEM	WEIGHT (lbs)	MOMENT/1000
Aircraft N-1234	1,182	88.25
Pilot and Passenger	295	25.50
Rear Baggage	10	1.00
Fuel	180	13.50
Total Weight 1,667	Total Moment/1000 128.25	

At 1,667 lbs, weight is within limits.

Again, total moment (/1000) is divided by total weight (/1000):

$$\frac{128.25}{1.667} \;=\; 76.93 \text{ (inches aft of datum)}$$

Now the resulting CG position is plotted on the Weight and Center of Gravity Envelope to ensure the loading is within limits.

As you can see using the Loading Graph has resulted in a slightly different Center of Gravity position, (as a result of rounding the moments up and down). As long as the result is still well within limits this is not a problem. If you get a result that is very close to the edge of the envelope, it is worth using the mathematical method to get a more exact center of gravity position.

A WORD OF WARNING: As well as the safety aspect, operating the aircraft outside its weight and balance envelope has far-reaching legal and financial implications. Almost the first thing an accident investigator will check after an accident is the loading of the aircraft. If the loading is outside limits, the pilot is violating the Federal Aviation Regulations. In addition, both the aircraft insurance company and your personal insurance company will be unsympathetic when they know that the conditions of the Airworthiness Certificate (i.e., the flight manual limitations) were not complied with. As the pilot-in-command, the responsibility is yours alone.

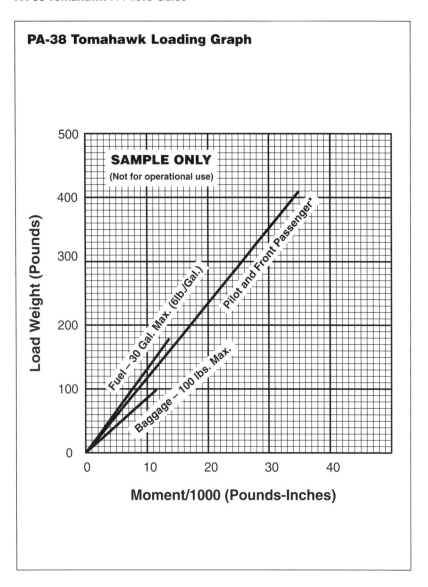

PA-38 Tomahawk Weight and Center of Gravity Envelope

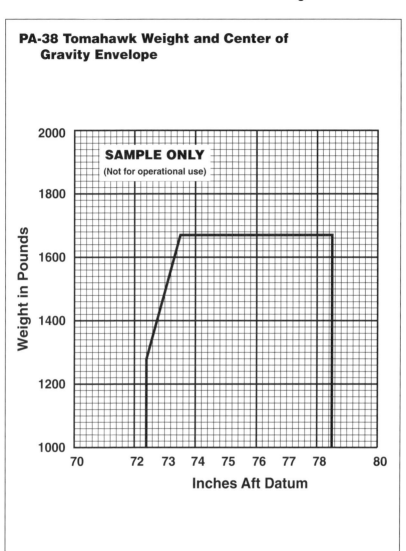

Performance

The Tomahawk flight manual contains a section of graphs and tables to allow the pilot to calculate the expected performance of the aircraft for different flight phases. The most commonly used graphs are those for takeoff and landing performance, and those are the ones we will concentrate on here. However, the same principles can be used on the other graphs. Two things to remember: First, the chart performance is obtained by using the recommended techniques—to get chart results, follow chart procedures. Second, you can safely assume that the graph results have been obtained by placing a brand new aircraft in the hands of an experienced test pilot under favorable conditions.

To make allowances for a less than new aircraft, being flown by an average mortal in real conditions, it is wise to "factor" any results you get. As with loading calculations, the pilot must use the graphs and data from the documents for the individual aircraft being used. The graphs and diagrams used in this section are for illustrative purposes only, and not for operational use.

In Section 7, conversion factors between feet and meters are listed, together with recommended factors for variations not covered by the flight manual graphs.

PA-38 Takeoff and Landing Performance Graphs

The takeoff distance and landing distance graphs in the flight manual make several assumptions (aircraft loaded to maximum gross weight; paved, level, dry, runway; use of flight manual technique). Different graphs may also be used for an aircraft with inboard *and* outboard flow strips, or with only outboard flow strips. The graphs here assume an aircraft fitted with inboard *and* outboard flow strips.

The graphs use the term "Pressure Altitude." This is the altitude of the runway assuming a standard pressure setting. On a day with a pressure other than 29.92" Hg you will need to adjust the actual altitude to get the pressure altitude. For instance, on a day with a pressure above 29.92, the pressure altitude will be less than the actual, and vice versa. To do this conversion, simply adjust the actual altitude by 1,000 feet for each inch Hg above or below 29.92" (10 feet for each .01 inch).

The headwind or tailwind component is calculated from the wind speed and the angle to the runway. That is, a 10-knot wind directly down the runway gives a headwind component of 10 knots; a 10-knot wind at 90° to the runway gives a headwind component of 0. There is a graph in Section 7 for calculating head/tail wind component and crosswind component.

The takeoff distance and landing distance graphs will state the technique used to obtain the figures. Remember, to get graph results you have to use the graph techniques.

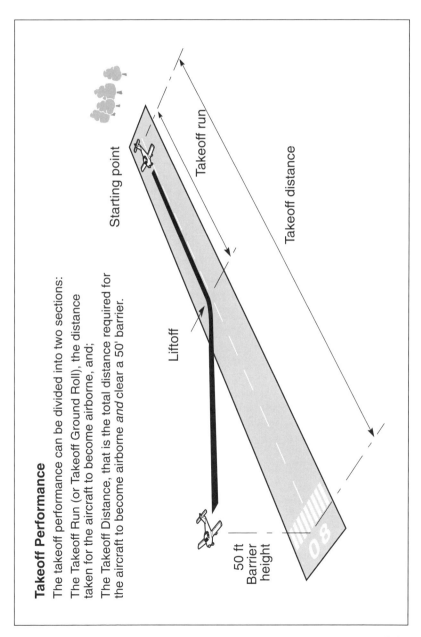

Takeoff Performance

The takeoff performance can be divided into two sections:

The Takeoff Run (or Takeoff Ground Roll), the distance taken for the aircraft to become airborne, and;

The Takeoff Distance, that is the total distance required for the aircraft to become airborne *and* clear a 50' barrier.

Starting point

Takeoff run

Takeoff distance

Liftoff

50 ft Barrier height

Takeoff Distance Calculation Example

For this example we will take the conditions as:

Outside Air Temperature +10°C
Pressure Altitude 1,000 feet
Headwind Component 10 knots

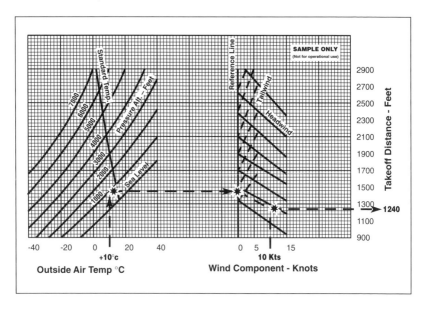

Start on the takeoff distance graph at the temperature of +10°C, and then go vertically to the pressure altitude of 1,000 feet. From this point go horizontally to the REFERENCE LINE, and then along the headwind guideline until above the 10 knots point. From this point take a line horizontally to the far side of the graph and read off the takeoff distance in feet, 1,240 feet.

Landing Performance

The landing performance is calculated as the Landing Distance, that is the total distance from 50' over the runway to a full stop. The Ground Roll (or Ground Run)—the distance from touch down to full stop—may also be calculated.

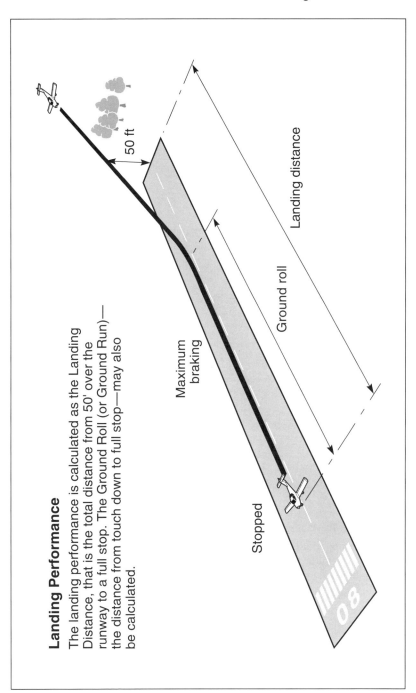

Landing Distance Calculation Example

For this example we will take the conditions as:

Outside Air Temperature +20°C
Pressure Altitude 1,000 feet
Headwind Component 4 knots

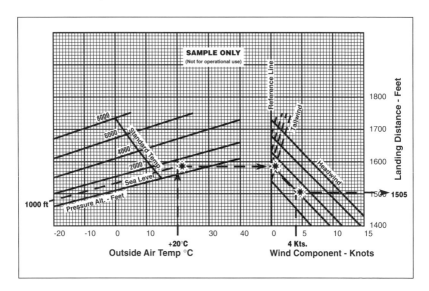

On the landing distance graph again, start at the temperature (+20°C)
and go vertically to the pressure altitude (1,000 feet). From this point, go
horizontally to the REFERENCE LINE, and then along the headwind
guideline until above the headwind component (4 knots). From this point
go horizontally to the far side of the graph and read off the landing
distance in feet—1,505 feet.

En Route Performance

Data is also provided in the flight manual for calculating the en route
performance, such as range and endurance. It should be noted that the
figures obtained in these charts rely on the use of the quoted procedures,
particularly the leaning procedures. If any other procedure is used, the
quoted performance is unlikely to be achieved.

PA-38 Takeoff Distance
Max Gross Weight, Paved Level Dry Runway

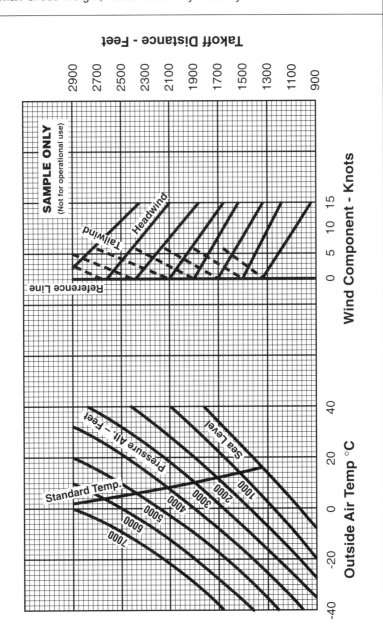

PA-38 Landing Distance
Max Gross Weight, Paved Level Dry Runway

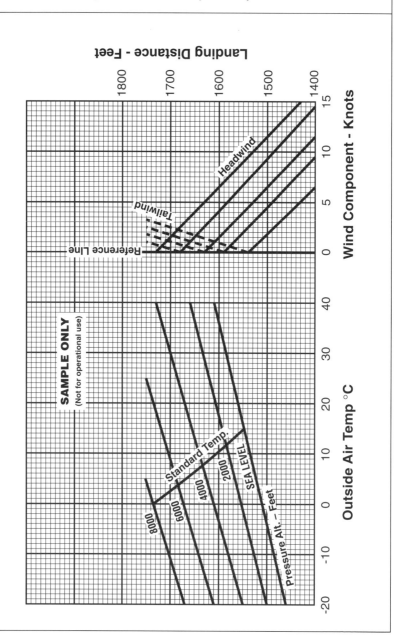

Runway Dimensions

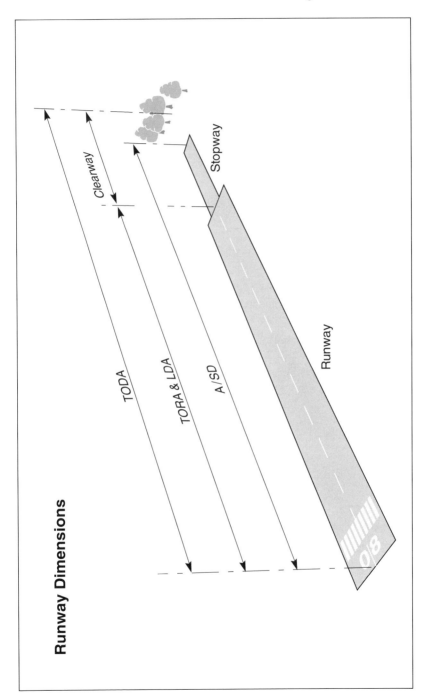

Runway Dimensions

Having calculated the distances the aircraft requires for takeoff or landing, the runway dimensions must be checked to ensure that the aircraft can be safely operated on the runway in question. The figures given in the A/FD or airfield guide can be defined in a number of ways.

The Takeoff Run Available (TORA)

The TORA is the length of the runway available for the takeoff ground run of the aircraft. This is usually the physical length of the runway.

The Accelerate/Stop Distance (A/SD)

The A/SD is the length of the TORA plus the length of any stopway. A stopway is the area at the end of the TORA prepared for an aircraft to stop on in the event of an abandoned takeoff.

The Takeoff Distance Available (TODA)

The TODA is the TORA plus the length of any clearway. A clearway is an area over which an aircraft may make its initial climb (to 50 feet, in this instance).

The Landing Distance Available (LDA)

The LDA is the length of the runway available for the ground run of an aircraft landing.

Section 7
Conversions

Takeoff Distance Factors

The following factors will allow the pilot to make allowance for variations that may affect takeoff performance. Although some of these factors are covered in the Tomahawk performance tables, the table is produced in its entirety for completeness:

VARIATION	INCREASE IN TAKEOFF DISTANCE (to 50')	FACTOR
10% increase in aircraft weight	20%	1.2
Increase of 1,000' in runway altitude	10%	1.1
Increase in temperature of 10°C	10%	1.1
Dry Grass		
—Short (under 5 inches)	20%	1.2
—Long (5 – 10 inches)	25%	1.25
Wet Grass		
—Short	25%	1.25
—Long	30%	1.3
2% uphill slope	10%	1.1
Tailwind component of 10% of lift-off speed	20%	1.2
Soft ground or snow *	at least 25%	at least 1.25
* snow and other runway contamination are covered on page 7-5.		

Landing Distance Factors

The following factors will allow the pilot to make allowance for variations that may affect landing performance. Although some of these factors are covered in the Tomahawk performance tables, the table is produced in its entirety for completeness:

VARIATION	INCREASE IN LANDING DISTANCE (from 50')	FACTOR
10% increase in aircraft weight	10%	1.1
Increase of 1,000' in runway altitude	5%	1.05
Increase in temperature of 10°C	5%	1.05
Dry Grass		
—Short (under 5 inches)	20%	1.2
—Long (5 – 10 inches)	30%	1.3
Wet Grass		
—Short	30%	1.3
—Long	40%	1.4
2% downhill slope	10%	1.1
Tailwind component of 10% of landing speed	20%	1.2
snow *	at least 25%	at least 1.25

* snow and other runway contamination are covered on page 7-5.

Runway Contamination

A runway can be contaminated by water, snow or slush. If operation on such a runway cannot be avoided additional allowance must be made for the problems such contamination may cause—i.e., additional drag, reduced braking performance (possible hydroplaning), and directional control problems.

It is generally recommended that takeoff should not be attempted if dry snow covers the runway to a depth of more than 2", or if water, slush or wet snow covers the runway to more than 1/2". In addition, a tailwind, or crosswind component exceeding 10 knots, should not be accepted when operating on a slippery runway.

For takeoff distance required calculations, the other known conditions should be factored, and the accelerate/stop distance available on the runway should be at least 2.0 x the takeoff distance required (for a paved runway) or at least 2.66 x the takeoff distance required (for a grass runway).

Any water or slush can have a very adverse effect on landing perfor-mance, and the danger of hydroplaning (with negligible wheel braking and loss of directional control) is very real.

Use of the Wind Component Graph

This graph can be used to find the head/tail wind component and the crosswind component, given a particular wind velocity and runway direction.

EXAMPLE:

Runway 27

Surface wind 240°/15 knots

The angle between the runway direction (270°) and wind direction(240°) is 30°. Now on the graph locate a point on the 30° line, where it crosses the 15 knot arc. From this point take a horizontal line to give the headwind component (13 knots) and a vertical line to give the crosswind component (8 knots).

On the main graph overleaf the shaded area represents the maximum demonstrated crosswind component for this aircraft. If the wind point is within this shaded area, the maximum demonstrated crosswind component for this aircraft has been exceeded.

Note:
Runway direction will be degrees magnetic. Check the wind direction given is also in degrees magnetic.

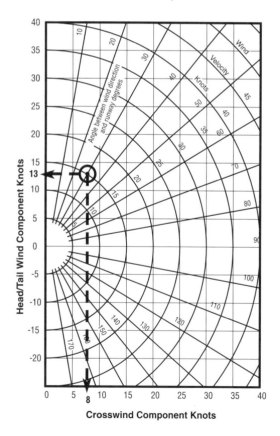

Wind Component Graph

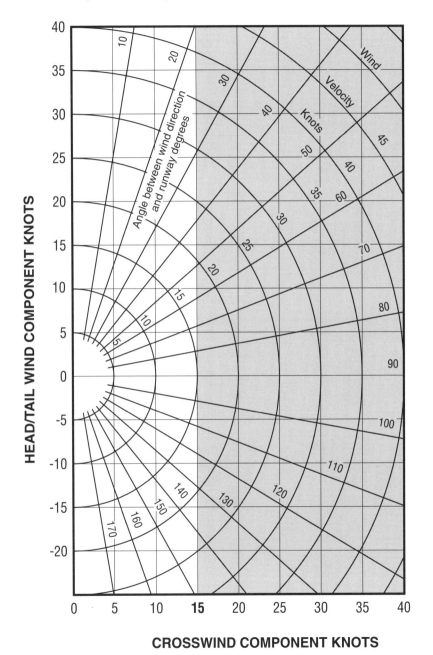

CROSSWIND COMPONENT KNOTS

Temperature

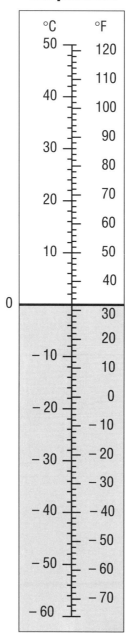

Distance – Meters/Feet

Meters	Feet		Feet	Meters
1	3.28		1	0.30
2	6.56		2	0.61
3	9.84		3	0.91
4	13.12		4	1.22
5	16.40		5	1.52
6	19.69		6	1.83
7	22.97		7	2.13
8	26.25		8	2.44
9	29.53		9	2.74
10	32.81		10	3.05
20	65.62		20	6.10
30	98.43		30	9.14
40	131.23		40	12.19
50	164.04		50	15.24
60	196.85		60	18.29
70	229.66		70	21.34
80	262.47		80	24.38
90	295.28		90	27.43
100	328.08		100	30.48
200	656.16		200	60.96
300	984.25		300	91.44
400	1,312.34		400	121.92
500	1,640.42		500	152.40
600	1,968.50		600	182.88
700	2,296.59		700	213.36
800	2,624.67		800	243.84
900	2,952.76		900	274.32
1,000	3,280.84		1,000	304.80
2,000	6,561.70		2,000	609.60
3,000	9,842.50		3,000	914.40
4,000	13,123.40		4,000	1,219.20
5,000	16,404.20		5,000	1,524.00
6,000	19,685.00		6,000	1,828.80
7,000	22,965.90		7,000	2,133.60
8,000	26,246.70		8,000	2,438.40
9,000	29,527.60		9,000	2,743.20
10,000	32,808.40		10,000	3,048.00

Conversion Factors:

Centimeters to Inches x .3937
Inches to Centimeters x 2.54

Meters to Feet x 3.28084
Feet to Meters x 0.3048

Distance – Nautical Miles / Statute Miles

NM	SM		SM	NM
1	1.15		1	.87
2	2.30		2	1.74
3	3.45		3	2.61
4	4.60		4	3.48
5	5.75		5	4.34
6	6.90		6	5.21
7	8.06		7	6.08
8	9.21		8	6.95
9	10.36		9	7.82
10	11.51		10	8.69
20	23.02		20	17.38
30	34.52		30	26.07
40	46.03		40	34.76
50	57.54		50	43.45
60	69.05		60	52.14
70	80.55		70	60.83
80	92.06		80	69.52
90	103.57		90	78.21
100	115.1		100	86.9
200	230.2		200	173.8
300	345.2		300	260.7
400	460.3		400	347.6
500	575.4		500	434.5
600	690.5		600	521.4
700	805.6		700	608.3
800	920.6		800	695.2
900	1035.7		900	782.1

Conversion Factors:

Statute Miles to Nautical Miles x 0.868976
Nautical Miles to Statute Miles x 1.15078

Volume (Fluid)

Liters	U.S. Gal.
1	0.26
2	0.53
3	0.79
4	1.06
5	1.32
6	1.59
7	1.85
8	2.11
9	2.38
10	2.64
20	5.28
30	7.93
40	10.57
50	13.21
60	15.85
70	18.49
80	21.14
90	23.78
100	26.42
200	52.84
300	79.26
400	105.68
500	132.10
600	158.52
700	184.94
800	211.36
900	237.78
1000	264.20

U.S. Gal.	Liters
1	3.79
2	7.57
3	11.36
4	15.14
5	18.93
6	22.71
7	26.50
8	30.28
9	34.07
10	37.85
20	75.71
30	113.56
40	151.41
50	189.27
60	227.12
70	264.97
80	302.82
90	340.68
100	378.54

Conversion Factors:
U.S. Gallons to Liters x 3.78541
Liters to U.S. Gallons x 0.264179

PA-38 Tomahawk Index

Notes

Notes

Notes

Notes

Notes

Notes

Notes

Notes